D0604396

1/3

# Working Terriers

Other titles by J. C. Jeremy Hobson:

*Beagling*   (David & Charles, 1987)
*Small Scale Game Rearing*   (Crowood, 1988)
*What Every Gun Should Know*   (David & Charles, 1989)

# WORKING TERRIERS

## Management and Training

### J C Jeremy Hobson

**HOWELL**
BOOK HOUSE INC.

230 Park Avenue, New York, N.Y. 10169

First published in Great Britain in 1989
by The Crowood Press

**Published 1989 by Howell Book House Inc.**
**230 Park Avenue, New York, N.Y. 10169**

**Library of Congress Cataloging-in-Publication Data**

Hobson, J.C. Jeremy.

  Working terriers: management and training/
J.C. Jeremy Hobson
  144 p. 23 cm.
  ISBN 0–87605–836–5
  1. Terriers.  2. Working dogs.  I. Title
SF429.T3H56    1989
636.7'3– –dc19           88–34584
                    CIP
ISBN 0–87605–836–5

Photographs by J.C. Jeremy Hobson
Line-drawings by Aileen Hanson

Typeset by Consort Art Graphics  Exeter  Devon
Printed in Great Britain at the University Printing House, Oxford

## Dedication

To my grandparents: especially my
maternal grandfather from whom I
gained my love of animals and country
pursuits.

'Not for the lust of the killing
Not for the hate of the hunted
But because of the gift of our fathers
Their blood in our veins that flow'

# Acknowledgements

The Author is extremely grateful to: Anne Brewer, 'Tarsia Kennels'; Ian Rainbow, The Fell and Moorland Working Terrier Club; Phil Woods for providing some of the photographic material. Frank Pepper and the Parochial Church Council of St James's, Swimbridge, North Devon, for providing much of the material in the appendix concerning the Reverend John Russell.

It is not always possible to seek out new, relevant information and so thanks must also go to Geoff Worrall of Tideline books for permission to quote from Lucas's *Hunt and Working Terriers;* Sceptre books, a division of Time Life International Ltd, for some pointers found in *A Standard Guide to Pure Bred Dogs.* Special thanks to: Bill Sayner; Chris North; Richard Groghan (terrier man to Mr Goschen's hounds) and to David O'Connell for once again, supplying me with a seemingly endless list of contacts and telephone numbers, all of which have proved useful. To Kathy Turner who stepped in at the last minute and made an excellent job of transferring my longhand into a readable manuscript.

Finally, thanks to all those who have allowed me to photograph their terriers in all sorts of situations.

# Contents

# 1 The First Steps

Every breed of terriers has its own peculiar characteristics and within each breed every individual member is a character. It matters little whether the animal in question is nowadays bred so small that he could almost fit into your coat pocket as is the case with the Yorkshire Terrier; or so large that, despite the affix of 'terrier' (derived from the word 'terra' meaning earth) a dog such as the Airedale could never be expected to go to ground. What is, however, important to the owners of these individuals, is the fact that they give enormous pleasure through their very individuality.

They are amazing in their versatility and surely there can be no other group of dogs which have been bred with such a variety of sport in mind. From the 'ratter' to the 'badger-diggers', the terrier's popularity has continued through at least a couple of centuries of law changes, during which some of the dubious reasons for owning a terrier have quite rightly been outlawed. There is no longer any reason to possess an animal which will fight a fellow of his own breed, bait a bull or bear, or one which, provided the quarry is taken from its natural environment and has had its teeth knocked out, will tackle a badger, winning money for his owner in the process.

Nevertheless there are a number of useful and legal occupations which the working terrier can still pursue without, at the same time, getting the responsible terrier owner a 'bad name'.

Phil Drabble, the naturalist, broadcaster and author, writing to me in connection with this book, pointed out the fact that many members of the non-terrier owning public are ready and willing to point an accusing finger at anyone who keeps a working terrier. It seems that even legitimate, law abiding owners are changing '. . .to other breeds rather than be associated with the riff-raff who now keep lurchers and terriers. . .There is so much badger-digging that keeping working terriers entails being classed with the same unsavoury lot.'

I have had a family interest in hunting from an early age, when Sunday mornings were spent helping out local farmers who allowed us to hunt over their land, by taking terriers ratting around their buildings or (being in the Pennines) on to the surrounding moorland after foxes which were a direct danger to their spring-born lambs. More recently, I have been employed as a gamekeeper where, during the course of my career, I have seen terriers used to extract foxes from cairns on moorland when they are a serious threat to grouse stocks, or as useful beaters on a day after pheasants. I personally have not seen any increase in the type of person whom Mr Drabble describes but I do know that they exist.

I hope, therefore, that in compiling this book, I can help prevent any potential or existing terrier owners from falling into the disreputable category.

In an effort to cover the subject

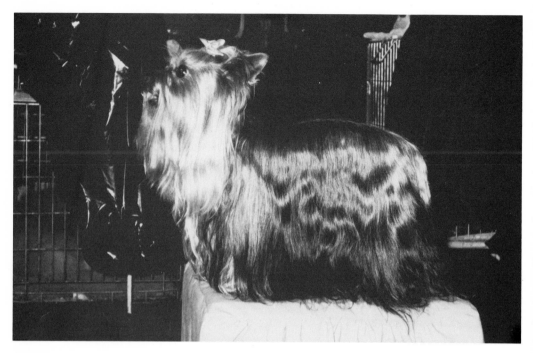

The Yorkshire Terrier was, when first originated, very much a sporting dog. Today, however, it is no longer classed in the terrier groups and is, instead, placed alongside the Toy breeds.

Terrier work is classed by some in the same way that irresponsible coursing enthusiasts are. (Purely out of interest, notice how quickly the whippet has noticed the hare move to the right of the photo.)

completely, this book, unlike some others which claim to deal with the working terrier, does not shirk some points which although necessary, may give offence to the outsider. It does, however, offer a balanced approach and, I hope, justifies what has to be done.

## ENTHUSIASM: PROBLEMS AND BENEFITS

That there is an almost fanatical obsession amongst terrier owners there can be no doubt, and this enthusiasm can be gauged in some little way from the comments written in the visitors book of St James's Church, Swimbridge, Devon where, for much of his life, the Reverend John Russell was the Vicar. Although a pretty hillside village and an unusual church, there is no doubt that it would have remained unknown but for the fact that its one-time parson was the originator of a particular type of terrier. Visitors from as far away as America and Australia have 'pilgrimaged' and written: 'Just had to come – I have a Jack Russell terrier'; or, 'Lovely church, splendid views, J R Owner'; or again, from Essex this time, no comment save that, 'I breed working Jack Russells'.

These are not, I am sure, 'badger-digging types' and probably the first two

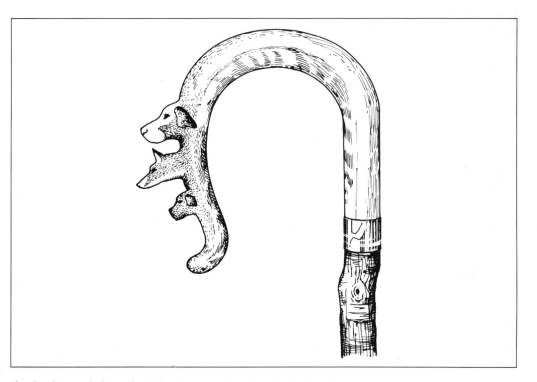

Shepherd's crook from the Lake District, depicting the heads of fox, hound and terrier, all carved from one piece of horn. It shows the interest in hunting and working terriers shared by most farming inhabitants.

comments of the three were penned by owners who are not even aware that terriers were bred to work – proving that terriers make excellent pets and companions. Terrier ownership is not, however, for those completely uninitiated in the ways of dogs, and to buy one without realising that certain breeds accept certain environments better than others is bound to create some unforeseen problems.

You cannot, for instance, buy a terrier simply because you have recently moved into the countryside and require some sort of sporting dog to enhance the image. You must first of all realise that, unless kept constantly supervised, a dog of this nature will very rapidly become accustomed to taking itself off into the fields and woodlands, following all the scents which instinct tells him that he should. Before very long he will be shot as a sheep worrier, buried alive whilst digging out a rabbit burrow or killed crossing a quiet country lane.

An urban environment causes as many, if not more, problems. Terriers are notoriously 'yappy' animals, barking if anyone even dares to tap on the front door of a house two streets away and if the owners are away for much of the time leaving the dog on its own, any undue noise will soon be commented on by the neighbours. Terriers, like some small people, can be very aggressive and will cross a road to pick a fight rather than avoid one, a fact which could prove very embarrassing when daily exercise is confined to park areas or walks where other dogs are frequently encountered.

Despite their small size, terriers need plenty of exercise to satisfy their inherited sporting instincts and if this is not given, the result will be a fat and possibly very disagreeable animal.

Left to its own devices a terrier could become buried whilst digging out a rabbit burrow.

Terriers are popular, but difficult – witness the fact that in 1985 (and possibly in more recent years) the terrier, especially the Jack Russell type, was the breed most often deserted, according to workers at Battersea Dog's Home. By going into ownership with your eyes fully open, however, there is much pleasure to be had from one of the working terrier breeds.

Their strength of character is probably first amongst their plus points. Working terriers which have been rescued from mountain crevices where they have been trapped for 21 days, or found 20 feet (7 metres) down after dynamite has been used to extract them, have, after a drink of water, been ready and willing to pursue the quarry which led them there in the

Terriers prove to be family friends as well as useful working companions.

said that it has been known for an older animal which is unused to children to be aggressive towards them.

Despite these facts it appears that although more are popular amongst the show fraternity, of the twenty or so breeds recognised within the Terrier grouping only a handful are popular with those who are looking for a good all-round working type.

## CHOOSING A BREED

Amongst this handful can be included the Fell breeds (Lakelands and Patterdales), the Border Terrier and the type originated by Jack Russell.

For someone who is interested in a ratting dog or rabbit catcher, rather than one which will go to the ground, there is also the Bedlington – but it must be said that for this type of work a lurcher created by crossing a Bedlington with a Whippet seems to be the ideal. Whilst on the subject of cross-breeding there are frequent references to 'Border x Lakeland', 'Lakeland x Jack Russell' or indeed any other combination in the 'Dogs for Sale' columns of the sporting or local press and these will, I am sure, prove to be every bit as efficient as a pure-bred. There is, however, a potential problem in cross-breeding as, in an effort to arrive at the best points of either breed, you are just as likely to pick up some of the worst ones. The quiet temperament of the Border may be lost in a cross between that breed and say, the 'harder' Lakeland. Crossing a show Sealyham with a Border, for instance, will only result in a merging and weakening of show and working blood in the offspring which will definitely be useless for showing under Kennel Club

first place. There have been reports of a terrier given to new owners in Surrey when the old owners moved to Norfolk, leaving home and seeking out the original owners at their new address even though the dog had never before been to the house. In the *Incredible Journey*, the author Sheila Burnford depicts 'Bodger' the Bull Terrier as being 'tough, with a strong sense of humour' and leading the way across the province of Ontario.

Any reader who has owned more than one terrier (the breed is immaterial), will already have realised the individualism of each animal, and the fact that although they may be closely related, they remain completely separate characters. They are usually loyal and protective especially when brought up within a family environment – although it must be

This fox was eventually bolted by the hunt's terrier man and survived to run another day.

rules and may be equally as useless when asked to face a fox.

You should be absolutely certain of the breed required and it is better to wait until an ideal puppy comes along rather than reluctantly choosing a second favourite breed because nothing else seems to be available. Eventually, if you wait long enough, the dog which you are seeking will appear either as a result of local newspaper advertisements or through the highly efficient terrier 'grapevine'. Starting with a substitute will never prove to be a satisfactory arrangement and even though the dog is bound to become loved and accepted, the initial relationship between terrier and owner will start off with the wrong vibes being passed between them.

Having briefly mentioned the buying of a terrier via the media, it is perhaps an appropriate time at which to point out that in an ideal world you should never need to buy a dog through these columns, relying instead on reputable breeders reached by word-of-mouth. Until you have been accepted into the 'terrier world' – and fortunately, this is easily achieved, its inhabitants being a particularly friendly bunch – this method of approach is impossible, and you may find yourself with no alternative but to look out for a dog which you have seen advertised. The majority of these breeders are very reputable, provided that you are not tempted into those 'puppy farms' where many differing breeds of dogs are reared for purely commercial reasons, but in all events try and take with you a person who is experienced with dogs (it matters little whether they know about terriers in particular).

More and more breeders are taking the very important step of keeping records connected with their breeding policies and this could prove useful to the newcomer who, as he inevitably becomes more enthusiastic, will perhaps want to begin breeding his own strain of a particular breed. Without such records it is impossible to ensure that a potential sire for your bitch is unrelated. Unlike show dogs which are registered with the Kennel Club and therefore possess pedigrees, there is no equivalent body to worry about the pedigrees of working types and so these records kept by keen enthusiasts are of great value. A person taking this kind of trouble with his terriers is more likely to produce good quality pups and should be visited in preference to one who does not.

# CHOOSING A PUPPY

One important factor when considering a pup from a particular litter is to make sure that it can do the job for which you wish to use it – even at the age of seven or eight weeks some 'gameness' should be apparent. Even within a litter of pups whose parents are proven workers, there may be one or even two individuals who, during the ensuing months, cannot be persuaded to enter and settle to any form of work.

If possible, see both parents doing the type of work which you eventually wish to do with your dog. If not, at least try and look at both sire and bitch as this will give you some idea as to how the pup will turn out.

Choosing a dog at seven to eight weeks is always something of a gamble but a few general points may help in making a decision. Many people suggest letting the brood bitch make the choice for you and this is done in the following way. First remove the bitch from the kennel and take out all the puppies from the bed, placing them in one corner. When the bitch is let back into the kennel, the dog which she picks up first should, according to those people who believe in this method, be the one which you take home. There is straight away a problem if she chooses a dog and you have your heart set on a bitch. If you have an animal of a certain sex already at home, it makes sense to pick a terrier of the same sex otherwise problems are bound to occur when the bitch comes on heat. When one is kennelled outside and the other is in the house this problem is lessened somewhat but always remember that a bitch in the prime time of her heat can be very devious and strong-willed when looking for a mate. At the

very least, a dog in the vicinity of a bitch in season, is likely to be quite vocal, especially at night!

You may not always have the option of choosing the best of the litter, as it is a common practice when the breeder does not own the sire to give the owner of the father, pick of the litter in lieu of stud fees. Also, if answering a newspaper advert, it is a safe bet that the advert will only have appeared because there is no other way of getting rid of the surplus and the breeder's friends will have chosen which pups they want before the advert appears.

Nevertheless, there is no reason why, provided that it is healthy, one of the remainder should not satisfy the first-time buyer. There are several points to watch out for and, on being shown the pups, you should ignore any which remain sitting quietly at the back of the box and concentrate on those who try to clamber out in order to take a good look at the stranger.

One puppy may immediately catch the eye and if for sale, should be the one to take home. First, take great care to check that he has neither an undershot or overshot jaw; that is where, when the teeth are closed, one set is either slightly in front or behind the other set. This is easily done by gently lifting back the lips whilst holding the jaws closed. At the same time check that the teeth are clean (and in a puppy they should be) and that the upper lip is pink, the latter fact usually indicating that the puppy is in good health. Clear, sparkling eyes are generally another good indicator as to the puppy's health. Remember also to ask whether the puppy has been wormed and what has been the usual feeding routine.

It is unlikely, unless you are buying a

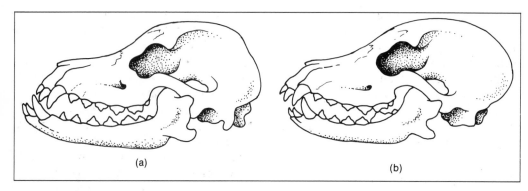

Examples of (a) undershot and (b) overshot jaws.

pup of ten to twelve weeks of age that it will have been inoculated but if it has, the cost of injections will have to be included in the eventual price of the dog. Inoculation is vitally important in all breeds of dog but especially so in one which is intended for working. Leptospiral jaundice (leptospirosis) can prove fatal to an uninjected dog which will come into constant contact with rats, who are known carriers of the disease. Some years ago parvo-virus caused an alarming number of deaths in young dogs but has, more recently, been controlled by the inclusion of the necessary vaccine in that required for the protection of hardpad, hepatitis and distemper.

As soon as you have bought the puppy, even though he may be too young for these injections, it will still pay to book an appointment with your veterinary surgeon so that he can give the dog a 'once over' and advise upon the best times to give the injections. Although vet's bills are expensive, they are nothing compared to the heartbreak caused by losing a dog through negligence, and the eventual cost of buying a replacement animal.

The chapter on breeding discusses in greater detail the feeding and rearing of a young puppy but the interim period whilst the puppy is growing can be profitably used to seek out a few useful contacts.

## FINDING SOMEWHERE TO WORK

It is quite likely that you have already got somewhere in mind for working a terrier. You may be employed as a gamekeeper and need a dog to help you cope with the fox earths situated on your estate; you may be a farmer or horse owner whose outbuildings frequently become infested by rats; or you may be someone already involved in the fox hunting scene with a good chance of helping out the terrier man of a particular hunt. It could be that you have been beating on a shoot and seen terriers as well as gundogs working and would like to try a terrier for this job — it is likely to be cheaper to keep than a spaniel or labrador and easier to kennel when space is limited.

In all these cases, finding somewhere to work a terrier is not a problem. If, however, you originally bought your terrier as a pet and walking companion but now feel that your dog's working potential is being wasted, you could find some difficulty, caused in part by those 'unsavoury' characters mentioned earlier, in finding somewhere to work him. Understandably, landowners are not going to be too keen on allowing a complete stranger free access to their land.

## Approaching Landowners, Keepers and The Hunt

You cannot approach a landowner and ask him whether he has any foxes that want digging out. Indeed anyone who intends keeping terriers so that he can go out looking for foxes to kill in this method purely for sport is, in my opinion, of somewhat dubious mentality and a type of person that I certainly would not wish to associate with. I know that parallels can be drawn with the hunting of foxes with hounds – they are, after all, to quote Oscar Wilde 'uneatable' – but at least with hunting there is a fair chance that the fox will get away, and members of the hunting field follow for other reasons than merely to see an animal killed.

It is perhaps better to approach either the local keeper or the hunt first, as by making contact with these people, the names of farmers or landowners likely to be sympathetic towards someone requiring a bit of rabbiting or ratting will become known. The best way of approaching the hunt is to find out the name of the secretary and try to get hold of a meet card. This may prove to be difficult, due to the adverse publicity enjoyed by the sport in recent years, so do not be surprised if hunt members are a little reluctant to talk to you on the telephone and even less keen to give you

their address so that you can put your request in writing. If you can give the name of a mutual friend as a reference, things will undoubtedly be made that much easier. On attending the meet, do not get in the way or be too pushy and you will soon be accepted. Join the Hunt Supporters Club if there is one and be prepared to help out at the kennels. There is much of interest to be learned by doing so, some of which could prove useful as you begin to work your terrier.

If you have an interest in shooting, the local estate may have vacancies for a few beaters to help out with driving the birds forward towards the standing guns. Some keepers do not allow the use of any dogs in the beating line, while others are only too keen for dogs to flush out game from the thickest covers. Understandably, the keeper will probably ask you to keep your dog on the lead for much of the time but in places which are very thick or which do not contain a vast amount of birds he will ask you to let your dog go.

Although not appearing to notice, the subsequent behaviour of the terrier will be noted and if he has proved useful, not only will you be asked to come again but there is a fair chance of being included on vermin drives at the end of the season. Then is the time for you to ask for a chance to do some rabbiting, either with ferrets and the dog or with the aid of gun and dog. It will be a very peculiar keeper who refuses such a request as any rabbits eradicated by other people lessens his volume of work, and prevents the farmer complaining about the amount of damage which the rabbits are doing to his corn.

Approaching landowners or farmers is still a difficult subject unless you have got to know them through hunting or

The end of a successful morning's ferreting.

beating, in which case they will know that you are a genuine sportsman and be more inclined to give permission for a walk around the hedgerows after rats and rabbits. Provided that you do no actual harm, I don't think that they will be too worried if you return back to your car empty-handed, but you must make a point of thanking them for their kindness in allowing you to go out. The offer of any rabbits which you may be fortunate enough to catch, or the occasional bottle of whisky will be enough to ensure that permission is always granted in the future.

The subject of terrier clubs is covered in Appendix 1, but by belonging to some form of organisation, it will show the outside world that you have at least a degree of responsibility and are prepared to do the job properly. Being able to say that you are a member of a particular club will probably allay any remaining fears which the landowner or farmer may have after your initial approach. There is a great deal of pleasure to be had from belonging to a terrier club. As well as shows organised for a working terrier, the social side is also very important and gives you the chance to make further contacts.

## SOME LESSONS IN DETECTIVE WORK

As a result of beating or following the hunt the terrier owner who has only recently been introduced to the countryside will have learned an enormous number of things and may have been shown the difference between, say, a fox earth and a badger sett.

Should the need ever arise for the enthusiast to dig out a fox it is essential that he should know the difference, as to in any way disturb a badger's home is an offence for which ignorance is no excuse. Having observed the two it is unlikely that any confusion will arise; the biggest difference being the vast volume of earth found outside a sett. Among this soil and debris will be found much short, straw-like vegetation which is the badger's bedding. Being a fastidiously clean animal, this bedding is changed on a regular basis, gradually forming a large platform. Some of these setts have been used by badgers continuously for many generations and have become very large as a result. The entrance holes are sometimes quite cavernous and drop down steeply. In sandy soil the clear prints of a badger are often noticed and, large though the hole is, the sides and roof are worn smooth by the constant passing to and fro.

Running your hand around the entrance, you will sometimes pick up badger hair, and it is almost certain to be seen in places where fibrous roots protrude.

The fox earth is somewhat different, although they will sometimes take over a badger sett, causing confusion as to which species is actually occupying the hole, and also make use of enlarged rabbit holes. Holes used by foxes are easily recognised especially if there are cubs, as the entrance becomes very worn. The foliage all around, (bluebells, grass and dog's mercury) is usually flattened as a result of the cubs playing and in wet weather will be covered in mud from their paws. Rabbits' feet and the feathers of birds (usually game), together with mole carcasses – which are never eaten, but used as playthings by the cubs – all indicate the presence of foxes.

A well-used badger earth is easily detected by the amount of spoil thrown out by the inhabitants. A clear set of paw prints can be seen in the freshly dug soil.

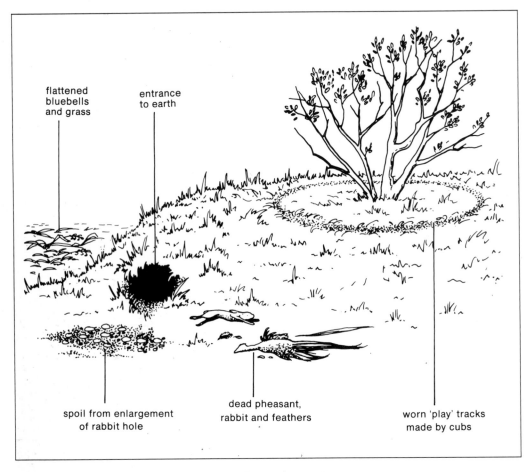

flattened
bluebells
and grass

entrance
to earth

spoil from enlargement
of rabbit hole

dead pheasant,
rabbit and feathers

worn 'play' tracks
made by cubs

When a fox earth contains cubs it is a relatively simple exercise to identify their presence by definite tracks to and from the hole, flattened grass and other vegetation, plus half-eaten carcasses left around the entrance. These are often used as playthings and dead moles seem to be a favourite even though they are very rarely eaten.

On bright May mornings there is often a heavy dew and if one of the parents has been out early, it will have gone back into the hole with a damp coat. On such a morning the air in the hole is so humid that the extra moisture from the animal's coat causes the entrance to steam. Well-established earths may be used by the same vixen in consecutive seasons, but it is more usual for them to breed in a different hole each year, only coming back to a previous earth after a longer period of time.

A good indicator as to whether a hole is currently in use is to look out for cobwebs across the entrance. Although they could have been built since the fox or badger returned home soon after day-break, the presence of webs generally means that the hole is disused. Tracks leading into the surrounding areas are made by both badgers and foxes but the ones made by the former, especially around a well-established sett, will be more immediately obvious. Possibly the most immediate give-away as to whether a hole is occupied by fox or badger, however, is the smell which emanates from a fox earth. It is a 'sickly-sweet' smell which, I am told, is not unlike that noticed when visiting wolves in the zoo. Badger setts do not smell at all (unless my senses have been so dulled by smoking).

A rabbit hole is, of course, obvious to all, but some of the ways of checking whether a fox is in residence apply equally as well when deciding whether or not a rabbit is at home. A lack of cobwebs, freshly-dug earth, recent droppings and, sometimes, patches of fur pulled out of the doe whilst attempting to mate are all useful indicators.

If you decide to look out for rats in order to train your young dog, the very heavily worn runs between piles of rubbish, sheds and outbuildings are usually noticed before the actual hole – which is, more often than not, perfectly round with little or no signs of digging.

## SOME PREFERRED CLOTHING

The terrier owner will in all probability already possess the more usual types of outdoor clothing and there is really very little to say on the matter of what to wear when working your terrier. To remain comfortable throughout an average winter's day, clothing should be reasonably weatherproof and easily movable. Nylon has several disadvantages and very few advantages: it creates

unnecessary noise and does not 'breathe', causing problems as you might be digging one minute and standing quietly the next.

Trousers of the corduroy sort are unsuitable, for they are apt to get soaked up to the knees and even higher in long undergrowth, and to remain soaked for the remainder of the day. Waterproof waxed cotton leggings are a good idea and will protect the wearer when beating, pushing through brambles for rabbits or kneeling down to listen for signs of activity underground from either ferrets or terriers. They also prevent much

Waterproof leggings are an integral part of the terrier man's wardrobe, especially when he carries his terriers on a trials bike! (Note the method of carrying the dog.)

mud from getting transferred on to what is worn underneath, but will need frequent replacing as the tiny granules of soil and dirt rub like sandpaper with the continual friction. Breeches or plus-twos which are not too tight at the knee seem to be the ideal legwear no matter what terrier work you are doing, and facilitate easy bending and kneeling.

There are bound to be prolonged periods of inactivity throughout the day and so it is important to wear warm clothing. Several thin sweaters are better than one thick one and the thermal underwear frequently seen advertised is immensely practicable. Wellingtons are probably the most useful form of footwear but if the ground is reasonably dry and there is much digging to be done, a pair of stout, well-soled boots will prevent the underside of the foot from becoming too sore as a result of putting necessary pressure on the spade.

# 2  Terrier Types

The British love-affair with the terrier probably originated from the fact that, during the nineteenth century, they were essential members of any working-class family who needed a dog, either as a destroyer of vermin or as a sporting ally. The minority upper classes fulfilled their hunting instincts by riding to hounds pursuing deer or coursing hares, but there was very little that the ordinary person could do in order to relieve the boredom of day-to-day life.

Perhaps not surprisingly when you consider the obvious monotony of a factory existence, inhabitants of industrial areas seem to have been particularly keen on possessing a sporting dog to enjoy during their limited leisure time. Together with cloth cap and white muffler, the whippet comes immediately to mind when thinking of the miners written about by D.H. Lawrence in *Sons and Lovers* but, with the exception of these and the packs of beagles or harriers

The Crawley and Horsham Foxhounds at Parham House on the occasion of Cliff Standing's last day as huntsman (1988).

Cats and terriers were useful vermin catchers in the stables and out-buildings which surrounded Northern industries. It is well worth taking particular note of the length, straightness of leg and broad fronts possessed by both terriers.

run by working men of the industrial north (who took to hunting at two separate venues twice daily in order that other factory workers on shift work could be sure of making at least one of the meets), terriers seem to have been the type most favoured. Their most obvious uses were in digging for either fox or badger or perhaps marking at a likely hole at which to introduce a ferret. Others, however, although they were called terriers, were involved in fighting sports which did not require an animal which could go to ground.

# RATTING AND FIGHTING BREEDS

## Staffordshire Bull Terrier

The Staffordshire Bull Terrier, as its name suggests, originates from the Midlands. This part of the country was rife with 'sport' which necessitated physical strength and endurance. Cock fighting and dog fighting were common sights on Sunday mornings, the arena being the boarded-in rectangle over which the spectators watched. Each dog fought to pull its opponent across a 'scratch' line drawn across the centre of the ring and any dog which failed to come 'up to scratch' was defeated. The Staffordshire Bull Terrier was developed for this purpose and no other with the result that dogs were so 'hard' that they would often fight to the death.

Another pit sport was that of rat-killing, and any type of terrier, provided that he was sharp enough, was used to see just how quickly he could kill a given number of rats in a certain time. There are many records still in existence, just two of which state that a black and tan terrier named Billy killed 100 rats in 7½ minutes at the Westminster Pit, whilst 'Jimmy Shaw's Jacko' was said to have finished off a 1,000 rats in an hour and a half.

Staffordshire Bull Terriers still possess the heavy head needed when they were bred as fighting dogs.

## Airedale

The Airedale, which was originally known as the Waterside or Bingley terrier before being credited with its present name, was derived by sportsmen in this area of Yorkshire to hunt out rats and other vermin from the slopes of the Aire Valley. Before the arrival of the German Shepherd Dog in this country, the Airedale was very popular as a guard dog with both the armed forces and the Police authorities.

## Bedlington Terrier

In Northumberland, the Rothbury terrier was crossed with the whippet and the Dandie Dinmont in order to produce a dog which was cheap enough to feed, hard enough to tackle rats in the local factories or steel foundries and fast enough to catch a rabbit. Unfortunately, the Bedlington, as this dog eventually became known, has today lost most of these working characteristics after being taken over by the show fraternity but it is occasionally possible to find a type such as the one illustrated here, which is capable of pulling down a rabbit. These few working types are much sought after by breeders of lurchers and long dogs in order to instill a little fresh blood into their own animals.

## Tibetan Terrier

As further proof that not all terriers were developed for work underground, the Tibetan terrier is officially classed as a herding dog, whilst the Cesky and German hunting terriers were farmers' dogs which combined a herding instinct with one which proved to be an effective means of vermin control.

Acedale Entertainer, a 20-month-old Airedale owned by Mrs J. Wallace. Bred by sporting Yorkshire-men, their present day looks are a result of an infusion of otterhound blood.

It is rare to find a true working Bedlington Terrier. This one, owned by Anne Brewer of the Tarsia kennels, is used regularly for rabbiting.

## Bull Terriers

Like his cousin, the Staffordshire, the Bull Terrier was bred as a fighter but became very popular amongst the colonials in the days of the British Raj, where it proved very useful in hunting deer and wild pigs. Around the owner's home it was efficient in eradicating the many and varied forms of vermin who found the cool environment under verandahs and raised floors very much to their liking.

## Manchester Terrier

Returning finally to the industrial north, another terrier which was evolved for fighting and competition work in the rat pits was the Manchester. The result of a cross between the old Black and Tan Terrier, which was common throughout Britain during the mid-nineteenth century, and the whippet, the new strain of dogs were, like the Bedlington, capable of both ratting and rabbiting.

## WORKING BREEDS

All the other breeds of working terrier in existence today are or were developed for their ability to go to ground after fox or badger. These 'real' terriers evolved long before fox hunting became fashionable and the need for a dog which would bolt a fox to waiting hounds occurred. Why they evolved, therefore, is something of a mystery, but, according to Guy N. Smith in *Sporting and Working Dogs*, 'animals similar in appearance to terriers were described in *Cynegetica of Oppian*', written circa 211BC.

Terriers have even been used by the Natural History Museum as a means of showing the various stages of canine evolution. (Devotees of the Staffordshire Bull Terrier would, no doubt, have much to say to the person responsible for mounting the right-hand exhibit!)

In the *Book of St Albans*, written in 1406, Dame Juliana Bernes mentions the terrier in her list of hounds, and Dr Caius described the terrier in 1576 as being:

'another sorte. . .which hunteth the Fox and the Badger. . .whom we call Terrars, because they. . . creep into the ground, and by that means make afrayde, nyppe and bite the Foxe and the Badger. . .'

Terriers are believed to have been in Britain since at least 1690 and there are records of the Gogeddon pack operating in Wales around 1696.

Nicholas Cox published *Gentleman's Recreation* in 1677, which although nothing more than a revamp of works written a hundred years earlier by Jacques du Fouilloux and George Turberville, nevertheless divided the terriers of his time into two groups: smooth-coated and short-legged, or wire-coated with long legs. It seems reasonable to assume in the light of these quotations, that it was only when fox hunting became popular during the mid-1700s, as a result of faster hounds and Thoroughbred horses being bred, that the need for a specific type of terrier arose.

Although every effort was made by the hunts to draw coverts specifically planted in order to provide a home for a fox, driving it towards open ground where it could be followed by the whole field and ending in a kill above ground, despite the best attentions of the earth-stoppers, foxes frequently managed to find an unstopped earth and spoil the run. Terriers were needed to bolt these foxes quickly and efficiently and it soon became a common sight to see small dogs capable of going to ground, accompanying the hunt, either on foot, or if there was much ground to be covered, in special panniers or sacks carried by an appointed terrier man.

Shire packs such as the Quorn, Belvoir, Vale of Aylesbury and the Duke of Beaufort were pursued by literally hundreds of mounted followers. In an effort to keep a hunt going at speed, thus pleasing those followers who really only wished to test the speed and jumping ability of their horses, the Duke of Beaufort produced a black and tan pack of hunt terriers around 1780. Whether this breeding was then used by others to produce the Black and Tan terrier described earlier which in turn led to the development of the Manchester terrier, is not known. Prior to 1780, the smooth-haired, short-legged dog mentioned by Nicholas Cox seems to have been the most popular type. It was completely white and was, from drawings of the time, not dissimilar in appearance from the type of Bull Terrier seen in books written around the turn of the century. By the mid-1800s there seems to have evolved three distinct types of terrier: the smooth, the rough and the Scottish. The first dog show to accept that there were now, in fact, three separate breeds occurred in 1862 when there was a class specifically for 'white and other smooth-haired English terriers except Black and Tans'.

Because game shooting was also becoming very popular, in particular the walking up of grouse on the northern and Scottish moors, gamekeepers were employed to ensure that the grouse had the best chance of survival. One way of doing this was to eradicate predators, and the worst offender was the fox. As no hunting was carried out, these keepers were at liberty to kill foxes by whatsoever means were available. Bolting them with terriers proved to be one of the most successful methods.

## Scottish Terrier

The name Scottish terrier did not, in the mid-nineteenth century mean only the distinct breed which we know today but denoted any type which was used and bred in the Scottish regions. H.D. Richardson, writing in 1853, refers to three varieties of Scottish terriers, one being 'sandy-red and rather high on the legs' and called a Highland Terrier. The second was the same size but 'with the hair somewhat flowing and much longer, which gives a short appearance to the legs. This is the prevailing breed of the Western Islands of Scotland'. The third was 'the dog celebrated by Sir Walter Scott as the Pepper and Mustard or Dandie Dinmont breed'.

Known for some years as the Aberdeen, the Scottish Terrier was originally more like a black Cairn without any of the exaggerated muzzle which is seen in today's specimens.

## West Highland White

Thompson Gray in his *Dogs of Scotland* (1891) refers to a visit made by a Captain Mackie to Poltalloch for the purpose of seeing a white variety of Scottish Terrier. The West Highland White was first called the Poltalloch Terrier and was, at one time, bred as the Scottish White. The modern 'Westie' is immensely popular, with well over 4,000 being registered annually with the Kennel Club. It seems to have survived 'improvements' thrust upon it by the showing fraternity, which is more than can be said for the Skye Terrier.

## Skye Terrier

Although once very much a working dog with a low-to-the ground build which enabled it to go to ground on either fox or badger, it is nowadays twice its original weight with a long flowing coat which would prove absolutely useless in protecting him either from the undergrowth or from the teeth of the animals which he once pursued.

## Cairn Terrier

Sometimes confused with the Skye Terrier because of the fact that they both originated from the Isle of Skye, is the Cairn. Said to be the smallest working terrier, it is a breed which has changed very little in the last 100 years and, as Dr Gordon Stables wrote in 1882:

'For pluck and pith and jaws and teeth
And hair like heather cowes,
Wi' body lang and low and strang,
At home in cairns or knowes.
He'll range for days and ne'er be tired,
O'er mountain, moor and fell;
Fair play, I'll back the brave wee chap
To fecht the de'il himsel'.'

## Border and Lakeland Terriers

Moving south out of Scotland you still find ground over which it would be impossible to hunt the fox with a mounted pack of hounds, so fell hound packs were established by the sheep farmers in order to rid themselves of animals which, though beautiful in their way, are very harmful to farming. Trencher-fed (that is kept by individual members of the various hunts), these hounds account for many dozens of foxes each year.

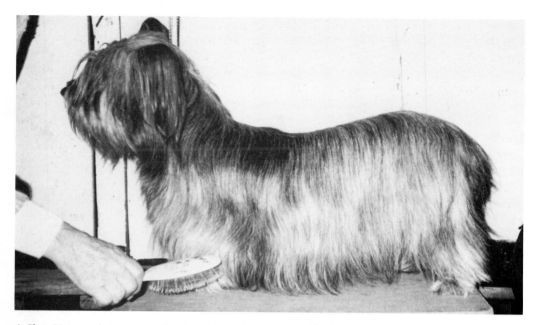

A Skye Terrier, the property of Mrs K. Loveday-Macdonald.
Thought to be one of the oldest terrier breeds, dogs fitting the
breeds description were known in Queen Elizabeth I's time.

Like the Skye Terrier, the Cairn was developed on the Island of
Skye and still looks a very workman-like animal.

Possibly the two types of terrier most commonly in use with these fell packs are the Border and Lakeland who, even now, are still expected to run with the hounds for most of the day. The stamina of these terriers can be gauged by a report which appeared in *Sporting Magazine* in 1818, stating that a pack of hounds hunted a fox for 8 hours, covering an estimated distance of 50 miles (80 kilometres)!

The Lakeland is the first (with the possible exception of the Cairn) of the breeds so far described in this chapter that is still flourishing as a working terrier. More correctly known as Fell Terriers, Lakelands, along with Patterdales and the rarely heard of Elter-

Watching and waiting. Not often seen is the 'red' Fell Terrier in the foreground.

water, are named after the area of the Lake District in which they originated. Like the Manchester, the black and tan colouring of the Lakeland came about as a result of crosses with the old English Black and Tan and is also thought by some to contain a certain amount of Bedlington blood.

As well as running with the hounds, the Fell Terriers have another thing in common with the Border. Unlike the rest of the country's working terriers, who are expected to work down to their quarry and then stand off barking so that the owners can pinpoint exactly where to dig, they are generally bred hard enough to stand up to the fox. There is a very good reason for this when you consider the topography over which they have to work. It is often impossible to dig through the rocks and crags of the fell districts and if a fox refuses to bolt it may be necessary for the terrier to kill its quarry underground. Also, unlike those southern packs of foxhounds who are able to stop up any likely earths the day before hunting is going to take place, there are often so many earths which cannot be stopped.

The photos of Mr Goschen's terrier man on page 72 show him with what he considers to be a Patterdale but when you see the emphasis put on the type of coat looked for in the fell breeds, surely this cannot be the case. The animal is very obviously smooth-coated whereas all the true fell breeds possess a hard, dense and wiry coat.

The Border Terrier gets its name from the Border Hunt where it was bred specifically to be both agile and brave enough to take a fox. According to Harry Glover's *Standard Guide to Pure-Bred Dogs* the rather powerful jaw is a result of the fact that the dog could quite easily

Border Terriers seem to have suffered the least from the attentions of the show fraternity and the average Border seems capable of tackling anything.

find himself facing the much rougher badger. The working variety still make very useful allies and I well remember nearly twenty years ago seeing a Border Terrier named Spider turning out with the Blencathra proving that the breed was more than capable of doing what they were bred for.

## Dandie Dinmont Terrier

Another dog from the Border regions but one which, although popular with the show world, is nowadays rarely if ever seen as a working dog, is the Dandie Dinmont.

Even those readers who have never seen a representative of this breed will, I am sure, know the story of how it came by its name. Sir Walter Scott, in the novel *Guy Mannering* named the hero of his story Dandie Dinmont and for some unaccountable reason, this dog which had, in its varied forms, been around the border counties since the early 1700s was re-named almost overnight. At that time, the breed was very adept at the hunting of badgers and otters as well as the fox and has, over the ensuing years, offered some of its blood in the development of other breeds. Owners of working Bedlingtons have cause to be grateful for this input as have the breeders of Sealyhams.

34

## Sealyhams

Sealyhams have (despite the fact that, from their overall appearance, they have not suffered too much interference from the show world), disappeared from the kennels of working terrier owners. Why this should be is not clear as, even as late as the 1940s, the Sealyham Terrier Badger-Digging Association had been formed in order to ensure that the sporting side was not ignored.

It is interesting to note that it was a Master of Foxhounds, Captain Jack Howell, who first got the Kennel Club interested in accepting the Sealyham to be a recognised breed. Whether he would have done so had he known that, in the late 1980s, the breed would only be known amongst show breeders, is open to question. One fact which cannot be denied, however, is that its earlier development came about as a result of cross-breeding with the Dandie Dinmont. Captain Howell felt that the soft topknot and large eyes found in a Sealyham invariably went with courage. These two points were undoubtedly brought about as a result of Dandie Dinmont blood.

As to the Sealyham's original formation it appears that, like many other breeds which owe their existence to the devotions of an individual, the Sealyham is no exception. Without the attention of Captain Edwardes of Sealyham House, Wales, this particular breed would probably have never come about as it was he who set about producing a 'short-legged, hard-coated terrier with a strong jaw and a white body, that would go anywhere and tackle anything'. Recognised by the Kennel Club in 1914, this marvellous breed originated by cross-breeding. His original cross was apparently a mixture of blood from the type of terrier which is nowadays known as a Jack Russell, the Welsh Corgi, some Bull Terrier and the Dandie Dinmont. Eventually, by select and careful line breeding, the Captain produced an animal which bred true to type and was by all accounts, very courageous. Captain Jocelyn Lucas, in his book *Hunt and Working Terriers* (1931), described Edwardes' methods of testing his young dogs:

'Captain Edwardes used to test his dogs on polecats. A drag was run to a covered pit containing a live polecat. This gave the terrier a little time to warm up. If he went in and killed the polecat, he was added to the pack, if he merely stayed outside and yapped, he was "put under". . . It was only by chance that Captain Edwardes discovered that Sealyhams sometimes develop their courage as they get older. One of his youngsters had been condemned, but was begged off by the farmer who walked him. Later on Captain Edwardes purchased him at a good price, for he turned out to be a really tip-top worker.'

## Jack Russell

The person most associated with the development of a particular breed must be Parson John Russell. Stories concerning him abound but, in this chapter of types and their evolution, it would perhaps be sensible to discuss the breed itself.

As you will see from the list of terrier clubs in Appendix 1, no other dog has led to so many disagreements and conflicts between various owners. Some feel that the breed should contain short-

A basic diagram which accentuates the differences between the type of Sealyham seen at the turn of the century compared to those seen on the show benches today. The legs have been bred shorter and the length of coat has been increased as has the heaviness of head.

legged, smooth-coated representatives, and others prefer long-legged and rough-coated animals.

The photograph on page 45 shows that Russell's first ever terrier was of the latter type, so surely this should be the ideal at which to aim? Although it is only a public house sign and could therefore be open to the accusation of artistic licence, it is in fact a reproduction of an oil painting which was said by Russell himself to be 'an admirable likeness'. The artist of the oil painting described the dog as being:

'White with just a patch of dark tan over each ear, while a similar dot, not larger than a penny piece, marks the root of the tail. The coat, which is thick, close and a trifle wiry, is well calculated to protect the body from wet and cold. . .The legs are straight as arrows, the feet perfect; the loins and conformation of the whole frame indicative of hardihood and endurance; while the size and height of the animal may be compared to that of full-grown vixen fox.'

Apart from the fact that they have divided the breed into two heights, The Jack Russell Club maintain standards which, I am sure, would not have displeased the Parson. The head should be strong-boned, have a powerful jaw, dark eyes and V-shaped ears, whilst the body should be straight with a high-set tail at least four inches (ten centimetres) long. Coats can be smooth or broken but should not appear woolly, and the overall colour must be white. Although most breeders are keen to ensure the continuation of the eye and tail markings found on the original dog, many do not object to hound-type markings.

Thankfully, then, today's Jack Russells are almost as they were when, in May 1819, Parson Russell saw and purchased Trump from a milkman in the Oxfordshire village of Marston. In the intervening years, however, the breed has been much abused. The original dog bought by Russell was a Fox Terrier which, although nowadays popular in France, is rarely seen as a working dog in Britain. (If you look at photographs of Fox Terriers from the turn of this century, however, you can see the modern-day Jack Russell, so perhaps one has replaced the other.) Since then, smooth-

A seven-month old, rough-coated Jack Russell type.

coated nondescript terriers have been added together with bull terrier blood, although such a cross made the breed too hard. Out crossing to beagles, Sealyhams and almost any other breed which could possibly introduce something new seems to have been the order of the day, with the result that terriers of indeterminate history, old-fashioned non-pedigree fox terrier types and any little short-legged terriers all became known as 'Jack Russells'.

## Wire and Smooth Haired Fox Terriers

Closely connected with the development of the Jack Russell is the Fox Terrier. The basic stock from which both the smooth Fox Terrier and the wire Fox Terrier descended was probably what might be termed 'half coated' as it was neither rough or smooth. This is especially noticeable in an engraving by Reinagle in *The Sportman's Repository* (1820).

The modern, smooth type originated circa 1860 and was probably helped in its evolution by the English White Terrier which has been mentioned earlier in this chapter in connection with the development of other breeds. Most of these developments can, in the absence of any recorded evidence, be based only on supposition but it is thought by many that the old, black and tan rough-coated terrier was used to produce the coat of the modern wire-haired variety. By judicious crossing of the two types, both the white base colour of one and the hard coat of the other were retained.

Very much in evidence as hunt terriers during the first three decades of this century due to their ability to run with the hounds, their popularity began to wane shortly afterwards but not before some of their good qualities had been bred into the modern-day Jack Russell.

## Norfolk Terriers

There are two breeds of terrier which, like the fox terrier, are today only ever found on the show bench but yet have not been so 'improved' by those breeders that they could not prove useful as working terriers. Why, therefore, are Norfolk and Norwich terriers rarely found in hunt kennels? When they first became known in the middle of the nineteenth century, they were used for hunting both fox and badger and proved very popular with the young undergraduates of Cambridge who, it was said, used to smuggle them into their lodgings so that they could enjoy a little vermin hunting along the banks of the Cam during their frequent breaks from studies. The dogs were known to be capable of drawing a full-grown fox from an earth and were also occasionally used as gundogs, but they really came into their own when ratting and rabbiting. In the early part of this century, they were called Trumpington Terriers and it was not uncommon to see markings of black and tan. Since they have become recognised by the Kennel Club, however they are only ever seen in 'red'.

A man named Jones, a horse dealer from Market Harborough, had a great deal of influence on the breed and when, after the First World War, several Norwich Terriers were bought by foxhound kennels in America they became known there as Jones Terriers. The only distinguishing feature between the Norwich and Norfolk terriers concerns their ears: the latter possesses drop ears; the former pricked ears.

The show-bred Welsh is very similar to the show type Lakeland. Old prints which originated in the eighteenth and nineteenth centuries show black and tan terriers not unlike the Welsh terrier of today.

## Welsh Terriers

Another breed which, because of its similarity to the Lakeland, makes one wonder why it too is not popular with working terrier owners, is the Welsh Terrier. Like so many of the medium-sized animals around today, it is almost certainly descended from the rough-coated black and tan terrier of the late 1700s early 1800s. It was, however towards the end of the nineteenth century before it was first seen as a pure breed on the show bench and, prior to this, used to run with packs of Welsh hounds bolting foxes from the crags and slate of North Wales.

## The Irish Breeds

Moving across the water to Ireland, you will find three breeds of terriers. Firstly, the Irish itself, the show type – there is no separate working breed surviving. This has a colour varying from wheaten to red and a size described as being '. . .between the Lakeland and the Airedale'.

The Kerry Blue is, apparently, an excellent guard, a successful herding dog and most surprisingly, a competent all-round gundog. The final true Irish breed is the Soft-coated Wheaten, which is believed to have played a part in the evolution of the Kerry Blue. Like the Kerry Blue, it was once expected to prove its worth amongst the Irish farming community during the days that a good all-round dog was essential.

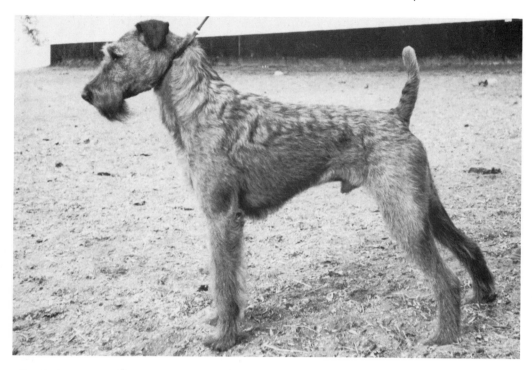

The Irish Terrier should ideally be red, wheaten or yellow-red in colour, and between Lakeland and Airedale in size and height.

Vermin needed to be eradicated, stock required rounding up at frequent intervals and, because of the isolation of the majority of Irish farmsteads, property needed protecting. I almost wonder whether such dogs couldn't, with a little training, be persuaded to cut and carry peats for the fire!

## A FINAL COUNT

I have, believe it or not, described twenty-three breeds or types of terrier within this chapter and should, perhaps, have mentioned the Dachshund, it being used at one time to bolt badgers. Interestingly enough, however, because of the fact that it was originally bred to

hunt by scent and then follow its quarry underground, it is recognised as being part of the Hound group amongst canine *aficionados*.

Why then, given the fact that there are so many terrier breeds still in existence, are there only three breeds considered to be true workers, namely, the Fell Terrier, the Border and the Jack Russell? The blame cannot be put at the door of the show fraternity as, if anyone had been interested enough in working a particular breed, no doubt two distinct types would have evolved – as is the case with the English Springer Spaniel. Perhaps working owners found that Fell Terriers, Borders and Jacks fulfilled all requirements but, if this were indeed the case, why did the Sealyham continue to flourish as a working dog right up until the 1930s? Or, if the Fox Terrier was so useful, why did the Revd Russell feel the need to produce another type? In fact, why bother with separate breeds at all when all that was needed was for each area to develop a hunting terrier bred to a type most suitable for the topography over which they ran?

Of course, that is exactly what did happen. and how the separate breeds evolved, but it goes nowhere towards explaining the reason for the decline in some breeds and this is very unusual in any form of livestock breeding. Friesian cows have, for example, taken the place of the dairy Shorthorn because they produce more milk. Modern long-backed pigs produce more rashers of bacon than did the type once found in every country worker's sty, whilst sheep were bred to suit the climate and grazing found in varying parts of the country.

This last factor could help in determining the reason for the decline in popularity in certain breeds of terriers in different regions. The South came to favour a shorter-legged, broad-chested dog because most fox earths were rabbit warrens which had been adapted for use by the vixen due to give birth. The larger, more unapproachable foxholes of the North meant that the Jack became less evident and its place was taken by one of the fell varieties or a Border. The argument sounds quite reasonable until you remember that, as there has never been a short-legged fox, the length of leg is not important.

# POINTS OF THE TYPICAL TERRIER

## Legs and Height

A discussion of the general requirements of a typical working terrier, must begin with a more thorough examination of this business of the legs. Briefly, however, the theory is that leggy, narrow terriers will be able to enter a small earth more readily than one which is half the height but is over-broad across the chest or behind the shoulder.

An animal which will be an ideal all-rounder, and if expected to do a great deal of work underground, should not weigh more than about 18lb (8kg). (Border Terriers will obviously be slightly smaller than this.) The front legs should be as straight as possible, with the cat-like rounded feet seen on the best hunting hounds. The legs will obviously be muscular in appearance as they need to be capable of digging, scratching at roots and pulling the rest of the body along the underground tunnels.

## Depth of Chest

A broad chest is important as, together with a well-sprung rib-cage, it will ensure that there is plenty of room for the lungs and the heart. You will probably notice, when attending working terrier shows, that the judge will (or should) attach great importance to whether or not he can span the chest of the dog currently under scrutiny. By doing so, he is assessing whether or not the animal is capable of fitting into an 'average-sized' hole.

I found it interesting to learn quite recently that this 'spanning' of a dog by judges, or any member of the working

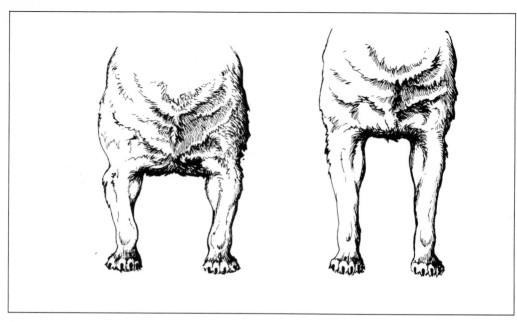

On the left is a result of irresponsible breeding: this terrier is
rather too broad in the chest and possesses 'Queen Anne' shaped
legs rather than the straight type described by most breeders. The
front of the dog on the right shows the difference.

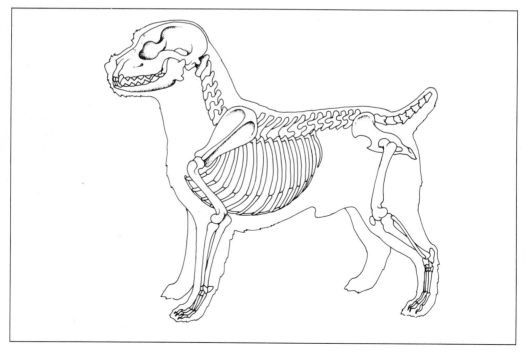

It is essential for a terrier to possess a deep, 'well-sprung' ribcage
in order to leave plenty of room for the heart and lungs.

## Tail Lengths

The Fell Terriers and the Jack Russells always have their tails docked in order to prevent any accidental injuries, but there has in the past, been a tendency on the part of some breeders to dock the tails too short. The second joint away from the base is usually considered correct and this will ensure that when the dog is fully grown, the tail length will be around four inches (ten centimetres) — long enough to provide a 'handle' when working but short enough to prevent injury. The tail carriage is also important and whilst it should not be carried vertically like a flag it should, nevertheless, give the impression that the dog is generally enjoying life.

## A Strong Jaw

At the opposite end of the body, it is obviously very important to a dog which could well have need to retaliate if a fox chooses to stay underground rather than bolt, that the jaw is strong and should not have the slightest hint of being either 'under' or 'over' shot. It is also generally felt that a terrier without a broad head cannot be expected to possess any brains. Indeed, Captain Lucas gave this as the major difference between the working Fox Terrier and that found on the show bench, saying that, 'the long, lead head of the dog does not allow for sufficient room for brains'.

## Coats and Colouring

On the question of coats, it is widely felt that the rough-haired Borders, Fell Terriers and broken-coated Jack Russells have an advantage over silky, smooth-coated dogs when it comes to with-

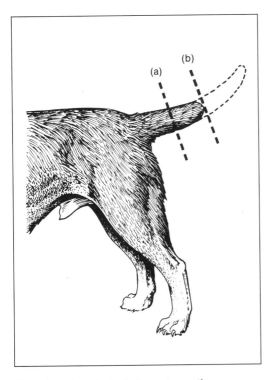

Many breeders dock their terriers tails at joint A but most prefer to dock at the second joint B.

terrier fraternity, originates from the fact that the terrier's chest should not be greater than that of a fox. As a dead fox is obviously a safer bet to test, and it is therefore assumed that a dead animal determined the span, it should be remembered that a live animal will have a slightly greater span. This is not only because of its natural air intake but also because any living thing will involuntarily take a sharp intake of breath when its feet are removed from terra firma. So, if it is assumed that the average *dead* fox measures fifteen inches (thirty-eight centimetres) around the greater point of its rib and chest area, one should not be too concerned to find that an average *live* terrier is an inch or two (two to five centimetres) broader.

standing wet or cold conditions, and for pushing through brambles. Also, if it is intended to do much underground work, a fairly thick coat may prevent the animal from getting quite so badly bitten. On the negative side, however, it is possible to overlook any resultant wounds. My own terrier, a rough-coated Jack Russell, had a disagreement with an Old English Sheepdog and nothing more was thought about it until, three or four days later, we noticed that a large, pus-filled, septic abscess had developed under the coat. Fortunately, with the minimum of care and attention, the wound soon healed but the incident proved just how easy it can be to miss any cuts and bruises. Some of these problems could be alleviated by stripping out the thickest of coats, leaving the harsh undercoat as protection but yet facilitating easy observation of marks in the skin.

Before it became common for hunt terriers to be transported by artificial means, smooth-coated terriers were often favoured in countries which contained much plough-land as they picked up the least amount of mud. Any dog which is continually going to ground, whether it be in possession of either a smooth or rough coat, is going to require some attention upon reaching home and, once the coat is dry, it is an easy matter to brush off the worst of the mud. The fact remains, however, that, for one reason or another, most working terrier owners prefer an animal with a broken coat.

The colouring of the coat is determined by the standards applicable to the individual breed and, in the case of the Jack Russell, which is not as yet recognised by the Kennel Club, most people adhere to the colouring set out as a result of the Revd John Russell's original dog,

Smooth-coated terriers pick up the least amount of mud.

'Trump': in her owner's eyes 'an admirable likeness'.

but, overall, the individual's working ability is more important than its coat colouring.

## BREEDS AND TYPES

Finally, I have throughout this chapter frequently referred to 'breeds' and 'types' and so an explanation as to the difference might be appropriate at this stage.

Generally, animals of a particular strain which conform to Kennel Club standards, due to the breeder deliberately selecting and using pedigree dogs which are known to throw certain desirable characteristics, are termed a true 'breed'. Most people refer to a 'type' when discussing dogs which, although mated together because of their favourable qualities, may produce some pups in the litter which are like neither parent. This is due to the fact that they have reverted back several generations to a point where blood from another line was introduced. For example, if, in the development of a certain type of Jack Russell, a Staffordshire Bull Terrier has been used in order to improve the shape of the jaw, the resultant litters may have had no trace of the Bull Terrier's particular traits for several generations until, for no apparent reason, a pup which is obviously descended from such ancestry, shows itself. Basically then, we talk of a Border or Fell 'breed', and a Jack Russell 'type'.

Trump. It is often said that hunt terriers without a sufficient degree of white on their bodies could be mistaken for the quarry by the hounds but, as the pack are held well back by the whippers-in whilst the dig is in progress, I feel that this is an unnecessary precaution. It is only when a terrier is to be used as a shooting companion that a predominantly white coat is advantageous.

A Border Terrier or a red, self-coloured fell type could, in the excitement, be mistaken for a fox or hare as they push through the cover towards standing guns

# 3  Early Days

Much of the work which a terrier is called upon to carry out is, by and large, purely a matter of instinct but, even in the best bred animals, it is usually necessary for the owner to channel these instincts from a very early age in order to achieve a biddable but competent worker.

Their basic early house training differs not one jot from any other breed of dog, but it must be admitted that terriers are notoriously dirty animals, especially when kept in a kennel environment and will not, unlike the majority of breeds, be as fastidious in keeping their sleeping quarters clean. I realise that this statement will probably cause howls of

indignant protest from those readers who keep a single terrier in the house, which has never disgraced itself since early puppyhood. Nevertheless I have, whilst speaking to many 'professional' terrier owners, heard this subject raised too many times for it not to be a true statement.

## BASIC TRAINING

### Coming When Called

It is important to make the puppy come immediately it is called and a prompt response may well save the animal's life

A traditional set of kennels which are not necessarily ideal for terriers, due to the fact that the size of the sleeping quarters encourages uncleanliness.

in later years. This training, in the majority of cases is easily achieved whilst out on exercise. You should occasionally call up the puppy by name, at the same time encouraging him by crouching down to welcome him. As soon as you see that the puppy is keen to scamper back to you, it may not be a bad idea to introduce him to a whistle. This is unusual advice in a book dealing with terriers but there is no reason why a terrier should not eventually respond to a whistle every bit as well as a gundog. It has a further advantage in that the sound of a whistle carries further than the average human voice – a fact which could prove useful when hunting through a wood or perhaps even when the dog has gone to ground. A small whistle with a high pitch is ideal; as you call up the puppy (from a crouched position) give a couple of short, sharp blasts on the whistle. At first, the dog will probably stop, unsure as to how to react to the new sound, but within a couple of days, most terriers will be coming to the whistle alone.

## Getting Used to the Lead

A lead, as in the training of any dog, is an essential part of the terrier owner's equipment and it is advisable to get your puppy used to the lead as early as possible. Do not, however, be too severe with him, as the idea at this stage is simply to get him used to the feel of something around the neck and the young puppy must not be frightened.

A couple of years ago, on the BBC programme *That's Life*, there was a clip of film which the audience found quite amusing, of a Yorkshire Terrier who, when taken for a walk on a lead by its owners, persisted in walking along on its hind legs, with one front paw holding on to the lead. In a following programme, the BBC had been approached by an ex-RAF dog handler who was concerned about the damage such walking would do to the animal's back and he offered to come in and break it of this 'hind-leg' walking. The cameras were there to witness the event and it soon became obvious that the dog was rebelling against the lead. By the use of a little canine psychology and holding the lead in a different manner, within a few minutes, the handler had cured the dog. If the owners had introduced the terrier to the lead in the manner which I am advocating, the problem would never have arisen.

You will never achieve the same amount of discipline with a terrier on a lead as you would with some of the other groups of dogs. Although, for the most part, a terrier is happy to walk at heel, if, as it becomes more experienced in later years, it pulls a little as it reaches a rabbit burrow or fox earth, this is perhaps to be expected. Some terrier owners expect and are pleased to have a dog which pulls at the lead as they feel that it shows their spirit but it is, in the main, much more comfortable for both dog and handler if the lead can be held slack. I once knew an owner of Staffordshire Bull Terriers who, for one reason or another, needed to keep his animals fit, and he used to give them plenty of road work. This, combined with the fact that they were encouraged to pull on the lead, built up very powerful chest and neck muscles which were, in the owner's eyes, very desirable attributes.

One final point on the subject of leads. A terrier not on a lead when approaching an earth will be down it before the owner has chance to stop him and if he has not had the opportunity of assessing the hole before this occurs, the dog may get severely injured. Also, it often happens that farmers or keepers use Cymag gas as a means of controlling rabbits or eradicating fox cubs and if this operation has recently taken place, a terrier which rushes in to the area can be killed with just one smell of this most dangerous of poisons.

## Sit and Stay

A terrier which has learned to stay is a useful asset and he can easily be taught to do so by a little training at meal-times. Hold the dish in your left hand (provided of course that you are right-handed) and, raising the right hand with palm held flat outwards say 'sit', 'stay', 'rhubarb' or any other command you wish to use. The first few times you attempt this, the pup will undoubtedly jump about in his excitement to get at the food but will eventually, sometimes by accident, sit down. Immediately he does this, put the food down and praise him. In a very short time, he will sit upon seeing the outstretched hand and, as time progresses, the period of time he has to wait before being given the dish can be lengthened.

Terriers are easily excitable and although this factor can be quite useful when you want to encourage a reluctant worker, without discipline the whole project is doomed to failure.

## Chastisement

If a young puppy does something wrong, he should immediately be told off in a very gruff voice but this can only be done if he has been caught in the act. There is no point in, for example, shouting and thumping a dog once he has returned to you after running off, as this merely makes him more reluctant to return to you the next time, associating the act of coming back, rather than the act of running away, with the punishment. It pays, in my opinion, to put the dog back in his kennel or, if a house dog, into his basket, for a few minutes after he has done wrong so that he realises that 'master' is not very happy. As with any dog you have to establish yourself as 'pack leader'; if you don't, the dog pretty soon will.

## Self Hunting

Any dog, but especially a terrier, should not be allowed to go off hunting by himself. If he is of a good working sort, it will not be long before he is hunting and, sooner or later, you are bound to lose him. He may go to ground after rabbits and dig deep in his effort to get at the occupants. It only needs a fall of soil to trap him and he will be suffocated.

If you live near a shooting estate, the terrier which goes off on his own is quite likely to end up caught in one of the keeper's fox wires, and although in the majority of cases, he will be found safe and well during the keeper's rounds, if a wire is set on a bank, the dog may slip down and strangle himself. If, after months of hard work on the rearing field, the keeper hears a terrier yapping through his coverts disturbing his newly-released poults, he may, understandably, shoot the animal and keep quiet. The worst danger of all, however, if a dog is allowed to hunt by himself is that, especially if he finds a companion of a like mind, he may eventually turn his attentions to livestock worrying. If this happens, you will have no alternative but to have the terrier 'put down'. Sooner or later, given half the chance, the farmer will do it himself, especially if the livestock in question happen to be sheep.

## Livestock Chasing

The prevention of livestock chasing and possible worrying should be considered during these 'early days' and is an important point even for those who merely intend to walk with their terrier in the countryside and have no aspirations of working their animal.

The best way to achieve this is by going to see a neighbouring farmer and first of all asking him for permission to take your terrier on a lead into fields which contain sheep. If the dog is remotely interested, pull on the lead and growl at him, possibly even tapping him across the nose at the same time. Should he still prove to be keen, try and get the

farmer to allow you to go right up to the livestock where the size and the noise of the animals may intimidate the dog. The terrier I have at the moment was a little too keen on the estate's sheep flock and so I tied her to the post of a gateway and drove some sheep through the gate. Although she seemed intimidated the first time through, I drove the small flock round a second time and, when she saw them coming, the terrier made every effort to pull away rather than, as she had been in the habit of doing, go towards them.

Various methods are used by farmers and hunt staff to ensure that their dogs will not worry sheep, the most common being that of putting a dog in close confinement with a ram, or a ewe which has just lambed and is, therefore very protective. This does not always work, however, as I once heard of a case where a hound was put in a box with a ram and

A pen of chickens is a good way of introducing a terrier to all forms of livestock.

left to suffer the consequences. On the farmer's and huntsman's return they found a very dead ram! Geese and chickens should also be encountered and if all possible eventualities are covered at an early age, there should be very little cause for concern. Do not ever be too complacent as you can never be totally sure of a terrier's temperament. A dog which regularly sleeps with the household cat could walk out of the door and kill the neighbour's cat which happens to be in your garden.

## TRAINING FOR SPORT

### Rats

Books on the subject of working terriers and every experienced terrier owner all agree on the fact that training a young terrier for sport should commence by getting it first of all proficient at killing rats. Most suggest that live rats are caught in traps and then either taken out in the trap to the middle of an open space or shaken out into an escape-proof loose box. After showing the young terrier the rats for a few seconds in order to get him excited, the door should be opened and the terrier allowed to get on with it. Others recommend that live rats are tipped into a barrel or a sack and that the terrier is thrown in and left to get on with it. Confining a terrier in this way is probably not going to do any good whatsoever and will, due to the lack of space available for him to turn around, possibly make the dog timid and unsure but will certainly result in him getting bitten by the rats.

A much more sensible and humane method of accustoming terriers to rats is

Ratting with a Jack Russell, and. . .

. . .with a Fell Terrier.

to locate some area where rats are to be found naturally. Any farm environment is obviously a good bet as there are plenty of easy pickings for the rats and good places for them to hide. Not only does the terrier get the opportunity to kill a rat but, by this method, may also learn to use its nose quicker than might otherwise be possible.

During the summer months rats are generally found to have moved away from buildings and taken up residence in the fields and hedgerows. If permission for a walk around these hedgerows can be obtained from the farmer, then presently your terrier is sure to mark a rat to ground. If he also 'speaks' to it, so much the better, but he should not be made too excitable or the time may come when he barks as soon as he sees a hole whether it is occupied or not. After a while, you can dig some of the soil away whilst the terrier is still marking and this gets him used to both the spade and earth falling about him. Any other holes which have been noticed should be blocked with soil or nearby suitable material to prevent the rats from bolting unseen.

In the winter, rats will move back into farm buildings and outhouses and, once again if permission can be obtained and you are sure that the terrier is steady to all forms of livestock which might be encountered, some good fun as well as invaluable experience can be derived from a 'mouch' about the farmyard. The inevitable piles of tin and fencing stakes are worthy of inspection, and it is worthwhile looking in disused outbuildings as rats can sometimes be caught there if the terrier is held quietly and released as soon as the door is opened.

Because my sheds on the rearing field are small and it is possible to tilt them forwards, these are an ideal way of training a young terrier, as the front tipping forwards forms a barrier from which a rat cannot escape, giving the terrier a little more time.

I would imagine that training young terriers with rats would have been a simple matter in the days when corn was stacked on the straw and then threshed out during the winter months. By all accounts, there was never any shortage of rats in the stacks, even though it was compulsory to surround the stack with wire netting to prevent an infestation. It must have been an interesting sight to see the threshers start their work and to see the men, boys, sticks and terriers waiting around within the netting compound. Most people, if they were sensible, tied up the bottoms of their trousers with string to prevent the rats seeking refuge in unwanted places! As the threshing began, the rats bolted steadily in ones and twos and were easily accounted for, but by the time the rick was reduced to about two feet high, things apparently became fast and furious. Geoffrey Sparrow, in *The Terrier's Vocation*, recorded killing seventy rats with one terrier.

There are a couple of final yet important points still to be discussed on the subject of rats. The first concerns the age at which to enter a terrier to rats. It used to be felt that, provided the rat in question was a young one, four months was an ideal time. Unlike many pontifications made 50 years ago, this adage still holds true and most modern-day terrier trainers insist that a pup must have his second teeth before being entered to rats. If a young dog gets badly bitten by a mature rat, he will never forget, and until he has his second teeth it is hardly fair to try him. There is a further complication as, before the second teeth emerge, any attempts at killing a rat may involve unnecessary and unsuccessful worrying. This could, in turn, result in the pup missing more than he kills, thereby boring the pup and giving him the idea that he will never be successful in killing his quarry. Where practicable, an older dog may help when attempting to enter a young pup but there is always the added danger that the 'employee' will be overwhelmed and over-excited by the 'employer'.

The second problem is Leptospiral jaundice, a disease of which rats are known carriers. In humans it is known as Weil's disease and can prove to be fatal. The same is true in dogs and so it is essential that a terrier which is likely to be doing a fair amount of ratting should be protectively vaccinated against this disease.

## Training to Respect Ferrets

It is perhaps more likely that the terrier will come into contact with ferrets when taken on rabbiting expeditions rather than when ratting as it is felt that using ferrets for this purpose tends to make them useless for any other work.

Nevertheless, if there is the slightest chance that your terrier will be used with ferrets, you should ensure that plenty of time is spent in introducing them. Those readers who own ferrets are in a slightly better situation to train their dogs – and possibly the easiest way in this case is to allow the ferrets to roam about when the pup is being fed. Filling its stomach is more important to most dogs than being curious about strange creatures running around the feeding area, and a young dog will soon learn to accept these

A terrier which is to be used as a regular rabbiting companion should be carefully introduced to the ferret before any serious operations are to be carried out.

intrusions even to the extent of allowing an inquisitive ferret to feed from the same bowl. Another alternative, for those with an older dog or infrequent access to ferrets, is to hold a ferret in one hand whilst restraining the terrier with another. Saying 'No' sharply a number of times when the terrier shows too enthusiastic an interest and giving soothing platitudes when it does not, will soon make the dog realise that the ferret is not to be tampered with.

When it comes to actually working with a ferret, the terrier should be kept on a lead for the first few outings. If a rat or rabbit bolts, he will soon take an interest in the quarry, which is quite acceptable and indeed should be encouraged. As the ferret emerges, however, some minor chastisement should be forthcoming if he shows more than a cursory interest. A dog should never be allowed to work at a hole while the ferret is underground in case he emerges suddenly and bites the dog. Understandably, the terrier will retaliate and could kill the ferret so it is obviously better not to let such a potential situation develop. Most experts suggest that a white ferret should be used whilst the terrier is in training as those of polecat colouring may be mistaken for the quarry until the dog becomes accustomed to them.

## Rabbiting with Terriers

Provided that the basic obedience training has been carried out from an early age and the terrier will return to his owner immediately he is called, introducing him to the joys of finding rabbits above ground is an easy task and one which the terrier will, in all probability, pick up for himself. The owner can assist where possible by noticing where

a rabbit has run into cover and putting his dog over the line which it has taken, allowing him to hunt the scent and flush the rabbit, encouraging him when he does so.

It should perhaps be mentioned at this stage that, having taught your terrier to flush rabbits, you cannot immediately rush out and fire a gun over the dog's head without first giving him a little experience of gunfire. The easiest way to do this is, again when the pup is still quite young, to make a bit of noise as he feeds and, if you are not situated in such a place as the neighbours will think World War Three has broken out, you could also stand outside and fire a shot. It has been suggested by those in the gundog world that a starter's pistol is a good idea to accustom a dog to the sound of gunfire but, in actual fact, the sound thus created is more in keeping with a rifle than a shotgun. When the latter weapon is subsequently used over the animal, he may find it a totally new experience.

Another alternative is to work the terrier around the edge of a field whilst a companion fires a gun at the opposite end. Depending upon the dog's reaction to the shot you can work up closer to the gun which is fired at intervals as you get closer. Experience gained from just being taken along on a lead and watching whilst ferrets are being worked will soon make the dog realise that rabbits generally live down holes and, as I have said elsewhere, it will soon learn to mark at burrows which are occupied and ignore those which are not.

If you are using nets rather than shooting then it will definitely pay to spend a little time in making the dog realise that the nets are there, otherwise it could prove rather frustrating for the

Terriers used for rabbiting soon become adept at knowing whether or not anyone is at home even before the ferret is entered.

It is essential to have a steady terrier which does not get in the way when digging or constantly rushes down the hole, disturbing the nets.

handler to be continually setting out the nets only to see the terrier stick his head down the hole and re-emerge with the net over his head Ena Sharples style! The terrier should also be prevented from dashing forward at the first sign of movement from within the hole as this is sure to make the rabbit less likely to bolt.

## Terriers as Beaters

As we shall see in more detail in the following chapter, a terrier can prove to be very useful either as a means of flushing game for the rough shooter or as a beater on the more formal type of shoot, provided that he is reasonably biddable.

The first requirement is that the dog will come back when called or whistled; the second is that he should not hunt too far ahead and that he should also quarter the ground on either side of the handler. A terrier which will not hunt through gorse, bramble and other thick cover is not worthy of the name and although some puppies seem to know that such cover is more likely to hold game than will an open expanse of bare farmland almost by instinct, others may have to be shown. This is not done by pushing or even throwing the unfortunate animal into the punishing depths of a blackthorn thicket, but by proving to him that it is good game-holding cover. Rabbits are an ideal way of achieving this but in their absence, some other means will have to be found.

Again, provided that he does not over-excite the youngster, an older, experienced dog will set a good example and a playful puppy will enter the cover for fear of missing something. I have also seen it suggested that a reluctant puppy can be encouraged into undergrowth in the following way. By letting the young terrier see you throw a biscuit or other favourite titbit into high but prickleless cover, at the same time telling him to 'get in', eventually, during the course of searching for the biscuit, the pup will find an interesting scent or even squatting game and he will soon realise what is expected of him. If it is possible to enter him into the wind, any scent will be carried towards him.

Having associated cover with something interesting and exciting, the next step is to get the terrier to hunt to right and left as you walk through the cover so that there is no chance of leaving any game undisturbed. Naturally, most dogs wish to run straight forward instead of quartering the ground but, by walking straight into the wind and moving from left to right yourself, you should soon be

An older, more experienced dog will set a good example.

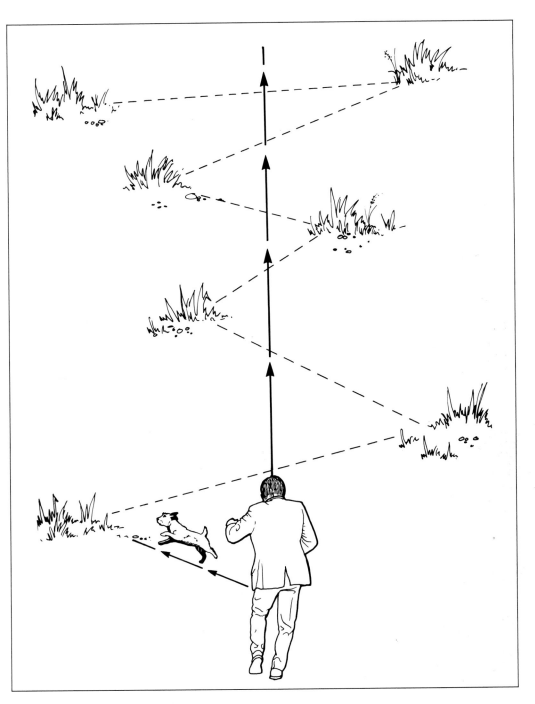

With some extra training it is possible to use a terrier successfully
when beating on a local shoot. Initial training should commence
by encouraging the dog to cover ground on either side of the path
which the handler intends to take. This is so much easier when
there are interesting clumps of cover for the terrier to explore.

able to get the terrier out beyond you in the direction across the wind that you are going. Further incentive comes from holding your hand out, preferably not very far from the ground, and verbal encouragements. As soon as he has got out to the distance that you require, call him or attract his attention by other means and turn towards the opposite side of your original line. As soon as the dog has come across and gone out in this new direction, call and turn again.

If it can be arranged so that, dotted on either side of your intended path, there are a few small clumps of bushes, bracken or bramble, the dog's natural inquisitiveness will make the task a little easier. But it is important to remember to allow the terrier sufficient time to explore these clumps: if you are in too great a rush the pup will skimp in his hunting for fear of being left behind. After a few lessons of this nature, you should have achieved two of the three things necessary for a shooting dog, namely, quartering and working your dog within a certain specified area.

The third requirement, that of not chasing game once flushed, is not so easy but is vitally important to those who wish to shoot over their dog if accidents are not to occur. If you can anticipate the break or flush by watching and listening to your terrier whilst he is still in the cover, it may be possible for you to put yourself on the side from which hunted and hunter are likely to emerge. By doing so, you should be able to shout a stern 'No', and maybe even catch hold of him. Praise him immediately afterwards and take him to hunt in the opposite direction so that he will not be tempted into going back to the original scent. Ideally, the terrier should sit as soon as he has flushed the game, as is the case with spaniels, but I think that this is carrying the trainability of even the most biddable of terriers just a little too far!

## Entering to Fox

You should never be in too great a hurry to enter a young terrier underground – his natural sporting instincts should first of all be developed by the means advocated earlier in this chapter. Most people agree that 18 months to 2 years is about the right time to commence this form of 'higher education'. Terrier owners differ greatly in their opinions as to how best to enter a young dog and so it is perhaps better to put forward all their ideas and let the individual make up his own mind.

The first possibility is to take the terrier out with the local hunt, as although he will not be allowed to participate in a dig, the pup will at least see the other terriers working, at the same time becoming accustomed to horses, hounds and all the general noise of a hunting day. Once the hounds and field have gone on, it may be possible to explain your situation to the terrier man who, once the fox has been shot, will, providing that there are no spectators, perhaps allow the young dog to worry the carcass of the fox. A shy dog may be frightened by too much vocal encouragement at this stage whereas a bold animal could get so excited that, when he eventually meets up with a live fox, he throws caution to the wind, rushes in and gets severely bitten.

Many other experienced terrier owners say that you should enter a young dog to a fox with the aid of an older accomplice. If the second dog knows his job, this will undoubtedly give the 'trainee' the right idea but could, in fact, result in him becoming so excited that he will rush in and get bitten by the fox. He could also, if the older dog is of a jealous nature (and in these circumstances, it would not be surprising if he were), get bitten by the terrier himself. Once this occurs, those two dogs will never again be able to be worked together, kennelled in the same run or transported in the same box. There are so many instances of terriers which have been together for months or even years, suddenly, as in the situation above, taking a dislike to each other and given half a chance, attempting to kill their one-time companion. For this reason, therefore, it is best never to work two terriers together down a hole.

Another method which works but which also has its disadvantages, is to let a pup face a fox once it has been located and dug down to. But without some sort of 'guard', such as a fork, which prevents either the fox from attacking the terrier or the terrier from rushing in at the fox, trouble is bound to occur and the dog is encouraged to attack. In the opinion of most people, it is more desirable for the dog to stand back and bark, giving the diggers an opportunity to dig down to where both fox and terrier are located.

Above all then, if for one reason or another, it is necessary to have a dog entered to a fox, you should take the whole business at a very gentle pace. I personally feel that it should only be necessary for hunts, farmers or keepers to own such a terrier, as digging out foxes for 'sport' in places where they are not likely to harm any lambs or game-bird stocks, is a rather dubious occupation. Land drains, pipes or even gaps between lengths of corrugated tin will all help the terrier to become accustomed to working underground and, as the group in general is naturally inquisitive, there should be very little difficulty in encouraging them to enter these dark places even though there may not be anything at home.

Finally, always remember that some terriers are slow to enter, but you should never be disheartened as some of these types have, in the past, proved to be excellent workers.

## NECESSARY EQUIPMENT

### Bleepers

If your profession necessitates the use of a terrier to work underground perhaps the most essential part of the equipment which should be readily on hand is one of the recently developed bleepers. For some time now, it has been possible to buy these bleepers for use when working ferrets, but until fairly recently, they had their limitations as far as being adapted for uses with terriers.

Bleepers for either ferrets or terriers are, apart from size, identical and work in the following way. A small, rounded transmitter, powered by a battery of the type found in hearing aids is fitted to a collar around the animal's neck. When the ferret or terrier is underground a signal is transmitted from the collar to a hand-held receiver above ground. This emits a 'tapping' sound, the rate of which increases as you move more directly above the animal. By first of all moving from, say, east to west over the area where the most rapid tapping occurs, then moving from north to south, the place at which the greatest noise is heard should pinpoint the exact location of terrier or ferret.

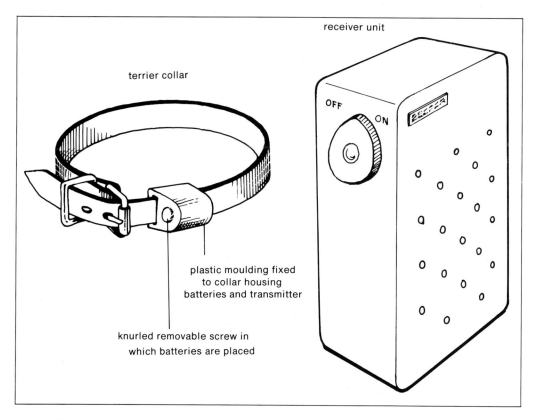

receiver unit

terrier collar

OFF

ON

plastic moulding fixed
to collar housing
batteries and transmitter

knurled removable screw in
which batteries are placed

A terrier bleeper and receiver unit. An ordinary collar is equipped
with a plastic moulding which contains both renewable batteries
and a transmitter. The terrier handler holds a receiver unit which
indicates the exact location of the terrier underground.

The reason why, until fairly recently, these bleepers had their limitations as far as terriers were concerned was that they would only transmit up to a depth of around six feet (two metres). Now the collar and units specifically designed for use with terriers are accurate to a depth of fifteen feet (five metres) – not, it is to be hoped, that you will ever need to dig to that depth, as fifteen feet (five metres) is a long way down! Nevertheless, when working in rocks and other impenetrable places it does at least give some indication as to where the terrier and the fox are located and you can begin to formu-late some idea as to what is happening underground. In the unfortunate event of the dog becoming stuck in rocks, the use of such a collar will give the diggers and members of the Fell and Moorland Terrier Club Rescue Team some point at which to begin their rescue work. In a situation where the terrier is lost over a long period of time, the batteries will, of course, begin to fade, giving a false indication as to the true depth.

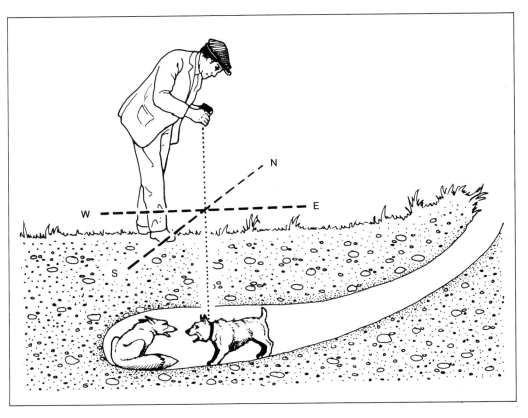

Using a bleeper. By moving the receiver in a north-south direction and then in a west-east direction, it should be possible to pinpoint the exact whereabouts of a terrier which is up against a fox.

## Netting a Fox Earth

It may, at some point during your life with working terriers, be neccesary to net a fox earth rather than is the more usual practice, stand back and shoot the fox as it emerges. There could be several reasons for this. The hunt terrier man could be asked to remove a troublesome fox by a landowner who, although he does not want the animal on his land, also does not wish to see it killed. Secondly, if a fox is bolted into a net it is a surer way than relying on helpers with guns who may miss with both barrels or,

worse still, hit but only wound the fox, allowing it to get away and die a slow death.

Another, purely hypothetical, occasion when nets could prove useful to some people is when a keeper or farmer has land which borders a place where foxes are known to be living and the owners of the ground will not give permission for him to enter the place. A 'dawn raid' with terrier and nets should catch the culprit without anyone being alarmed by the sound of a gunshot or even being aware of this clandestine visit.

The nets are bigger and made of

Fox nets are made of thicker hemp than those used for ferreting.
Their method of use is, however, exactly the same.

stronger hemp than those used for rabbits but are in all other respects, exactly the same. Operations should be carried out in a similar fashion to those which aim to catch rabbits. A major difference is of course, the fact that you cannot pull a fox out of a net and break its neck as you can with a rabbit. It has to be admitted that a swift, hard blow to the head with a spade will kill the fox but, if you are in possession of a firearms certificate and can get hold of a ·410 pistol for this purpose this is certainly a much more humane method.

Hunt terrier men will have a licence to hold a humane killer. Although it is in everyone's best interest to kill the fox as quickly as possible once it is in the net, obvious care must be taken to remove it away from the entrance to the hole itself if the terrier has not yet emerged. Depending on the size of the earth, this should not take very long and the terrier can be caught up and carried to a safe point before the fox is shot. Whether you then let the terrier go and worry the dead animal as its 'reward' is up to you.

## Digging Tools

The tools necessary when working your terrier to rabbits or foxes will vary according to the types of country over which you are working. In easy digging, perhaps only a spade is needed, whereas on land which contains a high degree of 'bargate' stone or sandstone, a crowbar and pick-axe will be required. Drainage rods, which will give an indication as to the length of a hole, or the point at

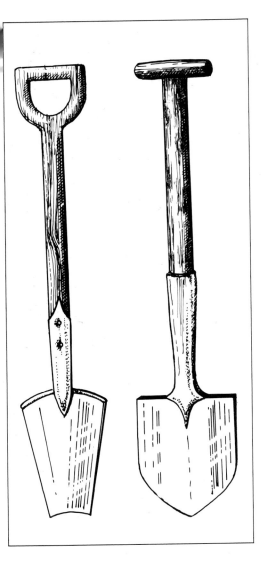

which it turns to either right or left, could prove useful although with the advent of the 'bleeper', the need for rods has, in many places, been negated.

Do not ever neglect to repair any damage which may be caused as a result of digging. It is obviously impossible to leave the place exactly as you found it, but every attempt must be made to 'make good' as near as possible otherwise not only is the landowner liable to refuse any requests for further permission but it is also unlikely that foxes or rabbits will return there in future years. With the former especially, you need to know the likely earth as quickly as possible when trouble occurs.

## TREATMENT OF WOUNDS

You should always carry a small first aid kit amongst your equipment and it is an easy matter to make one up which contains materials suitable for both dog and handler. Antiseptic solution such as TCP and cream such as Savlon, bandages, pads of non-adhesive gauze and waterproof sticking plasters should be the basic foundation of the kit and will contain all but the most serious of problems until either a vet or doctor can be reached.

Take great care to avoid any areas where rat poisons have been laid or strychnine has been put out for moles. Agricultural chemicals and dressed seed also form part of this group known as 'non-caustic' poisons. Washing soda which will induce vomiting has, in the past, proved useful when terriers have been unfortunate enough to pick up this type of poison but under no circumstances should it be given to an animal suffering from the effects of caustic

The right digging tools are essential when foxing, ferreting or ratting. A photo showing the full range of tools which may be necessary can be seen on page 64 but these two spades are especially useful. On the left is a grafting spade which, because of its curved blade, is invaluable in digging out tunnels whilst the one on the right is easier to dig with than are those with a flat-bottomed blade.

A selection of tools which may be needed by a professional terrier man. Note in particular, the bleeper and receiver in the bottom left-hand corner.

poisoning, having swallowed such substances as battery acids or barbiturates. Instead, the poison should be diluted whilst in the stomach by giving milk in the case of an acid or, for those of an alkaline nature, a solution of vinegar or lemon juice. In all cases, the idea is to prevent absorption into the bloodstream and is only an intermediate measure before seeking professional help.

# 4 Working the Terrier

How the varying breeds of terriers evolved is explained in Chapter 2 but one thing is for certain, they would never have reached their present form unless they were capable of earning their keep. They can, therefore, in a way, be said to be 'professional' and, although many are nowadays owned by people who choose to work them as a hobby or pastime at weekends, nevertheless, it is impossible to find another group of dogs which are so versatile.

Obviously much of the terrier's original vocation was in connection with fox hunting where they were, and indeed are, invaluable at bolting a fox from its earth. This is not the limit of their usefulness, however, and there are many working terriers which aid their owners even though they may never have seen a fox or its hole. Terriers are very definitely 'maids-of-all-work' and are especially useful to those people with an interest in shooting.

## SHOOTING COMPANIONS

Despite what the majority of non-terrier owning people feel about the 'trainability' of a terrier, it is, with time and a dog of the right temperament, possible to train a terrier to be every bit as steady and dependable as any of the more usual gundog breeds. Indeed it must be admitted that not every representative of these breeds is a paragon of virtue and can be every bit as headstrong as any terrier.

Terriers cannot, of course, be expected to retrieve an animal or bird once it has been shot, although I have seen some making a very valiant attempt. Their true value comes in the hunting for and flushing of any potential quarry. On the rough shoot, provided that the animal has been trained to hunt within gunshot – and by this I mean somewhere within thirty to forty yards (thirty to forty metres) of the guns – it should be possible to shoot at anything which the dog flushes.

One important aspect of the terrier's training if it is to be used for this purpose is steadiness, as, on the rough shoot, if a dog puts up a bird or animal and then immediately begins to give chase, there is the obvious danger of the Gun accidentally shooting his dog. If early training of the type suggested in the previous chapter is carried out, this should not cause too great a problem. For some reason, it seems that terriers which become accustomed to working with the gun show a greater inclination to point than do some of the modern gundog breeds. This is an attribute which should be encouraged by the owner who intends to use his dog mainly as a rough shooting companion – the delay will give you time to prepare yourself for the best possible shot.

I have seen terriers used with great success by beaters on the more formal shoots where game is driven towards a line of waiting guns. Because of their size, terriers of any breed can push through thick cover which may defeat even the keenest of spaniels. But, once again, although keeping within gunshot is not as important in this type of shooting work, at the very least the beater should be able to call or whistle his dog back at times when the gamekeeper demands it. There may be several reasons for this. When the pheasants are released, there are bound to be certain woods which do not contain that much undergrowth and so, as the beaters begin to push forward towards the guns, birds will run through rather than fly as they would if flushed from thick cover. Even if there is no cover at the beginning of the drive, a competent keeper will have ensured that there is a plentiful supply at the end, from which the birds are to be flushed. In this case there is the obvious danger of a terrier which cannot be called back rushing through to the end of the woods and flushing the game which is congregating there in one single hit. Such activities will not endear the terrier owner to the keeper nor the keeper to his employer.

Some woods contain cover in certain places and not in others, so a terrier must be biddable in order that you can call him back to push through clumps of brambles. If the dog is doing his own thing elsewhere, you may have no alternative but to beat through yourself, creating a very apt example of the saying that 'there's no use having a dog and barking yourself', or, in this case, 'no use having a dog and beating yourself'.

Although not quite so important, another reason why the dog should come back immediately it is called is that at the end of the drive, it could prove quite embarrassing if your dog should choose to bolt a rabbit from the hedgerow nearest to the standing Guns and then disappear in hot pursuit. This will undoubtedly cause much amusement to both beaters and Guns and, as I say, will prove most embarrassing to you. If the rabbit is chased into a neighbouring wood which is next on the itinerary to be driven, those cries of amusement will, very rapidly, change into cries of abuse.

A further point worthy of mention within this section, concerns beating through areas of kale and similar game crops with a terrier. No matter how well trained the dog, it is almost impossible for him to hear any commands as he rushes about under the stalks and leaves of such cover. He may, without realising it, get too far forward, once again flushing game in one great lump. Also in kale, be on the lookout for rabbits which may encourage your dog to run on too far. The easy living afforded by crops such as the above, makes a high population of rabbits very likely.

## FERRETING WITH TERRIERS

If you prove to be a useful asset on the shooting day itself, there is no doubt that the keeper or shoot owner will look very favourably upon any requests you may make to go ferreting.

A ferreting party is incomplete without a dog and a terrier or a lurcher makes the best canine companion. If the keeper is agreeable, the terrier can first of all be used to work through any cover in the woodland surrounding the holes to be ferreted and the running rabbits either shot or bolted into the burrows, where the ferrets can then be loosed. Many ferreters feel that this activity is detrimental to the subsequent procedures as it makes the rabbits less likely to bolt, but I have found that the operation has very little effect. Provided that unnecessary noise is eliminated (that is, you try not to tread all over the tops of the burrows or shout more than you have to), using the terrier in this way will make sure that every effort has been made to control all the rabbits in this area – a fact which is likely to find favour with the farmer or tenant.

If you are bolting rabbits into nets rather than shooting them, it is inevitable that you will fail to notice all the holes. Once the ferret has been entered, it is equally inevitable that any rabbits at home will bolt via this neglected hole! A fast terrier may be quick enough to catch such an escape after which the hole should be netted. With experience of ferreting, it is not uncommon for a terrier to become adept at pointing out holes which are frequented by rabbits and also pinpointing the exact position underground where a ferret may be laid up. This is a fact which will prove useful if it is felt necessary to dig.

# MOUCHING

The word moucher was once used to describe a particular type of country person – usually middle-aged, for before that period in his life he was still felt to be acquiring the knowledge necessary for mouching. He would have begun this apprenticeship to this very unusual 'profession' in his boyhood days, probably by wandering through the countryside with a quiet dog and a stick, learning the ways of animals and birds and occasionally picking up the odd rabbit or gamebird.

During the year, there were different money-spinning schemes to which he could turn his attention, for instance, collecting moss and wild flowers which he could then sell on to the town florist. Watercress, wild mushrooms, blackberries and holly berries at Christmas all provided a certain income, as did the sharpening of saws, knives and lawnmower blades. It was inevitable that, on his rounds, he would take with him two or three rabbit wires which he could set as the occasion arose. One thing was certain, however: he always had with him a quiet dog. Both dog and master came to know the countryside very well.

During my schooldays, I suppose that I could have been classed as a moucher, preferring the company of my terrier and a friend's lurcher to that of a human. With a complete disregard for footpaths and private ground we would wander for miles chasing, but very rarely catching, the odd rabbit, or waiting till dusk before picking out a turnip from the field of the local farmer. Occasionally, we would just watch the activities of fox cubs which always seemed to be born at the edge of a nearby quarry.

I think, in fact I hope, that there are many terrier owners who have a dog for no other reason but to accompany them whilst engaged in a little mouching. As a gamekeeper, I am not suggesting that you wander from the rights of way or indulge in a bit of poaching. Enjoy the countryside but be careful enough not to let your dogs run wild around farmers' livestock or in the woodlands at the time when pheasant poults have recently been released. There is a fundamental difference between those people with an interest in and an understanding of, the

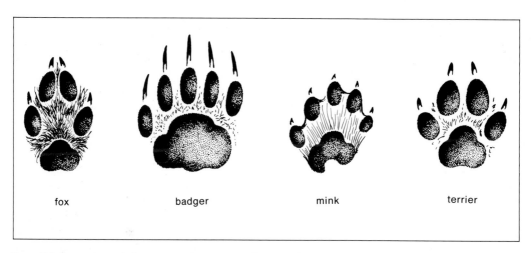

fox    badger    mink    terrier

Even if it is not intended to use one's terrier underground, it is still a worthwhile exercise to be able to identify footprints in the mud during a country walk.

countryside and those who merely visit at the weekend without realising the damage that an uncontrolled dog can do.

There is, therefore, immense pleasure to be gained from merely having a canine companion with sporting instincts, and a terrier is never content just to go for a walk. A bit of ratting along a riverbank; the amusing spectacle of seeing the dog jump with all four feet on to a clump of grass, only to observe a field mouse run out between his legs; or just to watch your terrier bumbling along with the obvious attitude of, 'Hang on, I've just got to have a look in here' — all of these make the whole business of modern-day mouching a much more enjoyable experience. For this reason it is, in my opinion, worthy of a part in this section on working the terrier.

## PROFESSIONAL TERRIERS

### As Keepers' Dogs

Most low-ground keepers have at least one terrier in their kennels and he is generally expected to perform a variety of duties.

He may be used in the beating line by the keeper, but tradition seems to dictate the use of a more orthodox type of gundog. Nevertheless, the terrier's versatility is put to full use throughout the remainder of the year and in the spring will be found accompanying the keeper around his traps and wires set to catch predators. Should a trap have failed to kill its captive, the terrier will quickly assess the situation and, with a single nip, do what the trap failed to do. (It must be made clear here that I am not talking of foxes caught in wires. For these the keeper should take with him either his shotgun or rifle. There is nothing kind or humane in letting a terrier loose on such an animal and, although it may be tempting to let a young dog 'have a go' this temptation must be avoided.)

At breeding time foxes frequently enlarge an existing rabbit hole in which to give birth to their cubs and if such an earth is found, the keeper will enter his terrier in order to pinpoint the whereabouts of the vixen. Once the fox has been located by the dog, it will either bolt, enabling the keeper to shoot it as it emerges or, if it refuses to budge, it is then possible to dig down to where the terrier is marking.

When the pheasant poults are on the rearing fields in mid-summer, the shelter afforded by the rearing huts and the close proximity of a ready supply of food will mean that rats are bound to take up residence. Although their runs are soon fairly obvious, and it may be possible to gas the increasing population, a terrier which will mark under a piece of tin or down a drainpipe and will then quickly finish off the rat subsequently found there, can help prevent an infestation before too much damage has been done. Likewise, in the food store, both rats and mice will be a problem, but I did hear of one keeper recently who left his terrier in such a shed whilst he went in for lunch. He was somewhat upset to find on his return that the terrier had managed to locate and kill a small nest of mice but at the expense of a tonne of rearing food which was now minus the bags and scattered into all four corners of the shed!

Once the poults have been released into the woodlands, it will not be long before they begin to fly over the release pen wire and wander off in search of natural food, despite the fact that the keeper is still attending the pens at least twice daily in order to feed them. The normal procedure when this happens is to carry out what is known as 'dogging-in'. Both morning and evening, the keeper attempts to walk his charges back to the pen. A terrier is ideal for this job as, if a gundog is used, not only will it make him somewhat unsteady and possibly ruin the poults' development, a gundog will tend to catch rather a lot owing to the bird's tendencies to crouch down in the hedgerows rather than fly off in the direction of home.

The grouse moor keeper is in a very different situation from that of his low-ground counterpart and his kennels are likely to contain more terriers than they will gundogs. Apart from the actual shooting day itself, you will see the moor keeper with his terriers rather than either spaniel or labrador due to the following facts.

Grouse cannot be reared and released so the whole operation relies on a good stock of birds and a successful, natural breeding season. There is very little the keeper can do to ensure this apart from burning off certain areas of his moorland in order to achieve varying heights of heather in which the grouse can either feed, take cover or nest. The second most important task is to rid the moor of predators, the two main ones being crows and foxes.

It seems, from my own observations made when I was employed as a beat keeper on the moors, that the fox's method when taking the sitting grouse is first to kill the bird and then eat the eggs before returning to devour the hen. If it is a vixen at work, the bird will most likely be carried away as food for her litter of cubs, so, if a broken nest is found, the keeper then looks around the nearest places which will offer a home to a litter of cubs. The easiest way to

Grouse moor keepers tend to use terriers on a daily basis, only working their gundogs on an actual shooting day.

destroy the foxes, once found, is by gassing them with Cymag, and this is usually the method used by the low-ground keepers. The moor keeper is, however, likely to be faced with a problem because most of his earths will be found in craggy rock formations. These cannot be gassed because the Cymag will escape through the numerous gaps in the rock before reaching the cubs. A terrier is the obvious solution to the problem but even then, although a single fox may be bolted and shot as it emerges, the method is never very satisfactory when dealing with cubs, because they seldom bolt and there is always a certain amount of doubt as to what has happened inside. The terrier may have killed all the cubs but it is impossible to dig through the rocks in order to find out

and any cubs which may have escaped will be led away by the vixen to another earth.

You cannot set snares for foxes on moorland because they have no obvious runs, unlike on low ground where they will use tracks through a wood or gaps in a hedge. So, as unsatisfactory as his methods may be, the grouse keeper has no alternative but to rely on terriers to help him in his 'war' against the fox. As his experience on a certain moor grows, the keeper will begin to find that some cairns and crags are favoured by foxes and are often occupied by more than one fox at a time. J. Spottiswoode, in his classic *The Moorland Gamekeeper*, observed this on several occasions and noted an instance where a Border Terrier, belonging to a local shepherd, had been entered in a rock formation above Redesdale valley and bolted five foxes before showing himself above ground.

## Hunt Terriers

Unfortunately for the interested amateur, it is nowadays very rare to find a Master of Hounds who, upon seeing a fox go to ground, will allow a nearby observer the opportunity to enter the terrier which he 'just happens to have with him'. At one time, however, a few foot followers who were known by the Masters and huntsman of a particular hunt to own trustworthy and reliable terriers would be allowed to try their animals if the official terrier man was engaged elsewhere. These people were known as runners and were especially useful in a situation when hounds had run a fox to ground, left the terrier man digging because the landowner or keeper had specifically asked for the fox to be killed and had subsequently marked another fox to ground. The hounds would then be held back by the whippers-in, and the runner's terrier entered to bolt the fox thus allowing the hunt to continue.

Although the act of fox hunting has changed very little over the years, the way in which terriers are used has, and, with the exception of the fell packs, it is no longer common to see them running with the hounds. The great drawback to this lies in the fact that it is frequently impossible to prevent the terrier going to ground unasked, thus forcing the Masters to embark upon a dig which they did not desire. Terriers in this situation are also very apt to riot and the presence of them hunting rabbits and deer in a covert through which the hounds are drawing is not calculated to increase the steadiness of any young entry which may be present. On the plus side, however, at times when the pack is unable to force the fox away from a very thick piece of young gorse or brambles, terriers running loose prove very advantageous as their small size enables them to get through even the thickest covert as quickly as the fox itself.

The types of terriers used have also changed over the years and it is nowadays unusual to find a particular hunt breeding a specific type of terrier. Occasionally this breeding policy is still being carried out, and today there is a stamp of black and white terrier on the Isle of Wight which is identical to a type found in hunt kennels in Essex. The reason behind this is very simple in that the breeding was carried out by one man, a terrier man to a certain pack who then moved to another. In the main, it is more usual to find the personal preference of either the terrier man or hunt staff being used although the breeds may vary according to the locality in which they are worked. Jack Russells, for instance, are known to mark a fox underground and stand off barking, either to let the owner dig down or give the fox an opportunity to bolt. In notoriously difficult digging areas, hunt terriers used in these situations must be powerful enough not only to 'bay and bolt' but also to kill, should the quarry prove impossible to move.

Most packs hunting over this type of ground seem to favour either the Border or the Lakeland. A good proportion of white colouring used to be an essential prerequisite of a hunt terrier, as it was felt that a darkly-marked animal was likely to be mistaken for the fox and get accidentally 'chopped' by the hounds or even, if the dig was being carried out by enthusiastic supporters, hit with the spade. Accidents do inevitably occur but nevertheless, dark-coloured terriers do not seem to provide the majority of hunts with any great cause for concern.

Another way in which terrier work differs now from that of say, fifty years ago, is that whereas at that time terriers would have been rarely used once the cubbing season was finished, today a terrier is almost as essential as the hounds themselves. It is this latter fact which explains why, even in these days of high wages and subsequent job losses, most hunts are prepared to pay for a professional terrier man.

## Terrier Men and their Duties

There can be no hard and fast rules when describing the employment of a terrier man and most hunts handle the matter in their own, individual way.

Some terrier men may, for instance, be employed as kennel men, combining day-to-day duties with that of running terriers on the hunting day. Others may, for the majority of the year, be employed by either the hunt committee or one of the Masters as a gardener/handyman, jobs which allow ample opportunity to work the terriers during the quieter winter months when hunting is in full

Richard Groghan, terrier man to Mr Goschen's Foxhounds, with two of his working terriers. (Note the fit and muscular appearance of both dogs.)

A Toyota Hilux is an ideal 'flesh wagon' used by several hunts and also proves to be a useful form of transport for the terrier man. Note the winch.

swing. Some of these 'professional' men receive a tied cottage as part of their employment agreement, whereas others may own property of their own due to an earlier, more lucrative career.

I also know of several hunts where the terrier man is a blacksmith by trade and is employed as the hunt's terrier man only for the duration of the hunting season. This is an ideal arrangement I would have thought and one which should ensure a ready supply of customers. In such a situation, it is likely that the terriers will belong to the individual rather than the hunt and also that he will use his own transport. If a Land Rover or similar four-wheel drive vehicle is supplied to the terrier man, at the beginning of the day he could be expected to fill up the back with fence posts, barbed wire, rails, staples and hammers as well as all the requirements necessary to dig

out a fox. Should the field damage the farmer's fences at any time of the day, then immediate repairs can be effected.

It is essential that the terriers turn up at a place where the fox has gone to ground as quickly as possible. It was once common to see a terrier strapped into a specially-constructed bag and carried over the shoulders of the terrier man, mounted usually on horseback but occasionally on bicycle, but there is no point in seeing the terriers arrive at great haste if the necessary tools for digging are a long time in arriving. Where possible then, terriers and tools should travel together in the back of a reliable vehicle. There are nothing but disadvantages in having a terrier man on foot or on a bicycle and it is doubtful whether any hunts use these methods today. Horseback is not much better as only one terrier can be carried. Secondly, it is

73

not safe for a mounted man to carry any sort of tool on his back even if he never goes faster than a trot.

If you look into the rear of a vehicle in which terriers are being transported, it will probably be found to contain a box split into several small sections, rather like those used for carrying ferrets. Obviously, the compartments are slightly larger but, ideally, each section should only contain one terrier. They should not give the occupant any opportunity to see out of either the side or rear windows, as the terrier group is notoriously hyperactive and highly strung. If they are transported as a pack it only needs the combination of a different environment and the diversion of a passing dog to set them off into a frenzied state of excitement, during which they may well start to fight each other, resulting in some very serious injuries. (Chapter 6 deals with this extremely important aspect of terrier ownership in much greater detail.)

## Digging

Before entering the terrier into the earth, you should ensure that both the tools

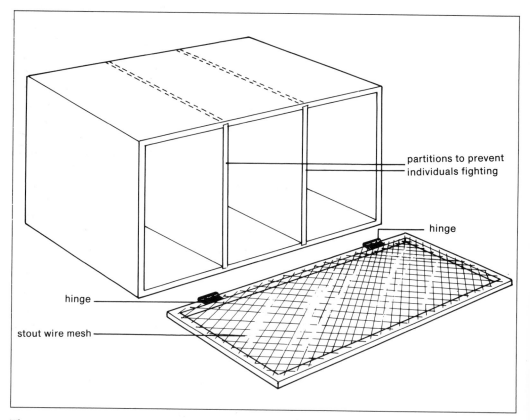

partitions to prevent individuals fighting

hinge

hinge

stout wire mesh

There are many ways of transporting terriers. This illustration shows an easily constructed unit suitable for three animals. It is important to isolate highly excitable canines.

and the men to use them have arrived, as there is no sense in having either the fox or the terrier unnecessarily punished. The quicker you can locate, dig down and remove both the fox and terrier the better, and the greatest care must be taken to see that none of your actions can possibly be construed as an act of cruelty by the casual onlooker. This is another reason apart from those already outlined why most Masters are not keen to allow amateurs to enter their terriers. It may, for instance, be necessary to dig for a fox whilst hunting over common ground or near to a public right of way, and it is not good policy to allow just anyone to work their dog to a fox in front of members of the public who may be opposed to field sports. It is better to have just one professional who is answerable to the hunt in the event of anything going wrong.

Locating a terrier which has marked a fox underground is much easier than it used to be as most workers of terriers have seen the value of the recently developed bleepers which do away with the need for any haphazard digging. In some circumstances, it may be necessary to revert to one of the more old-fashioned methods of digging, and in some cases, where the earth is so large that to dig by normal methods would just give the fox the opportunity of running around underground without the terrier being able to pinpoint and hold him in one particular area, it may be necessary to dig a large trench right across the middle before actually starting to dig towards the fox. The trench has the effect of splitting up the earth, thus making the whole operation more manageable.

Depending upon the area, some earths of great age can contain literally hundreds of yards of tunnelling. In one particular part of Surrey, on ground over which the Surrey Union hunt, there is, I am told, a tunnel at one of these earths, still in existence although it was dug nearly half a century ago by the terrier men. Apparently they tunnelled so deeply into the hillside that they were totally submerged and did not reach their fox until midnight (long after the hounds were back in kennels). When they eventually re-emerged into the 'outside world', the sweat which had been generated and had soaked through their clothes immediately froze due to the onset of a heavy frost. By the time they reached home, their outer garments were solid with ice. Such dedication is not normally necessary in the majority of earths but when, for one reason or another, it is felt advisable to use an old-fashioned method, a decision must be made whether to 'crown' or 'pipe'.

If it is decided to follow a 'pipe', rather than to risk the quicker but more uncertain method of 'crowning down', a stick should be kept in the pipe which is being followed, for fear of losing the tunnel and suffocating the terrier. From time to time the soil must be cleared away from the mouth of the pipe, and the terrier given air. If the tunnel is very narrow, it is quite possible that the fox will be blocking out any air which may be coming in from the pipe running out behind it and so this periodical clearing of the mouth of the pipe is absolutely essential.

## Earth-Stopping or 'Putting To'

One reason why terriers were not used quite so much fifty years ago was due to the fact that most hunts employed an earth-stopper as an essential member of the team. In the true heyday of hunting, when new hunts were building their kennel establishments they also erected buildings in which to accommodate the earth-stopper, his ponies, terriers and tools of his trade. The old earth-stoppers gradually disappeared: theirs was cold and hard work, and it was not very well paid. Their successors in nearly all hunting countries were the gamekeepers of large estates and even as recently as seventeen years ago it was part of my duties as a keeper's boy to block up any known fox earths when the hounds were due to visit the following day.

Earths are stopped so that foxes may be found above ground, and the process should be carried out in all the coverts in which it may be necessary to draw. Foxes do not leave their earths until dusk or even later and so, in the days when it was my responsibility, I was never allowed to begin earth-stopping until 9p.m. Although it seems that today's foxes prefer to live the majority of their lives above ground, they will of course go to ground on being pursued by hounds. With the increasing lack of anyone who is prepared to stop the earths, the terrier man is becoming an essential part of the set-up.

Because of the great interest in badgers and the new legislation outlawing any disturbance, intentional or otherwise, the Masters of Foxhounds Association have apparently suggested that any earths which are to be stopped and may contain badgers should be approached with the view to allowing badgers an easy exit. The best means of actually stopping an earth was always considered to be by the use of strong stakes and bundles of faggots kept permanently *in situ*, but now that badgers are protected,

the whole business of earth-stopping needs to be reconsidered.

## HUNTING DAYS

Despite the fact that the ordinary terrier owner will not be allowed to work his terrier with the local hunt, there is no reason why the enthusiast should not go along to a meet and watch the 'professionals' at work. Hopefully, the following notes will assist you as a newcomer at a meet of foxhounds.

Charles Willoughby, encouraging people to *Come and Hunt* (1952), suggested that the novice should

'keep a keen eye on the man he will see there with a couple of terriers on a lead; for it is his business to keep in close touch with hounds all the time they are out. From a well-disposed terrier man much can be learned.'

Today things are not quite so simple and it is unlikely that a stranger can approach a hunt and expect to be made immediately welcome. Obtaining a meet card outlining the forthcoming venues is now almost an impossibility and long gone are the days when you could see such a card sellotaped to the saddler's shop window, pinned to the pub notice board or set out in the advertising pages of the local press. It should, however, be possible, provided that you are dedicated enough, to track down someone who is associated with the hunt establishment.

Generally, foxhounds meet at eleven and, apart from needing to know that you should never interfere with hounds or get in the way of a potential scent, there is very little to be told. There is much to be learned, however, and, like

Unfortunately, hunt protesters seem to be taking an interest in any form of hunting with dogs and this includes terrier work. It is, however, more usual to see such people out with the hunts.

Charles Willoughby, you could do worse than attach yourself to the terrier man. Once he realises that you are a genuine enthusiast and what is more, keen on terrier work, it needs to be a very dour person who will not share *his* enthusiasm with a fellow terrier owner.

## Mink Hunting

Many old books deal with terriers in connection with the digging of badgers and the hunting of otters. As the hunting of both species is now quite rightly illegal, it might be supposed that the use of terriers in these 'sports' is not applicable to a book of this nature. Mink hunting has, however, taken the place of otter hunting and much of what was written then applies equally as well to those terrier owners who are fortunate

enough to live within travelling distance of a mink hunting pack.

'Jack' Russell used his own stamp of terriers to bolt otters from their holt, and there is no reason to suppose that terriers of the type which he developed should not be equally at home in flushing mink from their makeshift home along the riverbank. Jocelyn Lucas, in *Hunt and Working Terriers*, described the activities of Miss Alice Serrell, who hunted otters with a pack of old-fashioned fox terriers: 'The otter was facing him [a dog called Racer] and the two collared each other at once, with the result that the dog drew him.' The bite of a mink, like that of an otter, is worse than even that of a fox or badger, and it needs a special breed of animal to combat a mink in its home environment.

Otter hunting was never as formal a

sport as foxhunting and was always considered very much a 'love and lunch' affair. Once it became illegal to hunt otters, packs of minkhounds were soon formed (some of the old otterhounds providing the nucleus of the pack) and these, because they purely and simply exist to rid the country of its ever-growing mink population are concerned even less with formality. It might, therefore, be possible for the interested terrier owner to go along to one of their meets and get the opportunity to enter his terrier.

Unlike otters, mink do not have specifically built holts and instead only use holes in which to have their young. Obviously, if chased by hounds, they will use any form of escape available to them but likely places in which they have

their nests include hollow trees and holes in river banks especially in places where tree roots overhang. It can be reasonably assumed that they will use similar places in which to hide. Mink are hunted throughout their breeding season and meets are usually increased during the critical cub emergence period. Hounds and terriers properly entered can be amazingly efficient – such a combination can even account for mink which have escaped into a land drain and would normally have to be left if put there by the keeper or farmer with no terrier at his disposal. Contacting a local pack of minkhounds is, therefore, a very useful exercise on the part of the enthusiast.

Otterhounds of the type seen on the left of the photograph were also instrumental in the original breeding of the Airedale.

# FINALLY. . .

There is a school of thought which claims that, because of their fast metabolism, working terriers seldom make 'old bones' and there will undoubtedly come a day when, although the spirit is willing, the flesh is very definitely weak, leaving the professional terrier owner having to make a decision as to whether the dog should be retired or put down. This same school of thought, rightly or wrongly, suggests that it is better to have an old but sound animal destroyed sooner rather than later instead of letting it waste away through 'nerves' and inevitable metabolic changes within the body.

# 5 Showing the Working Terrier

As a result of becoming involved with either the local hunt or one of the many terrier clubs, you may be tempted into putting your dog forward at one of their shows in the hope of winning a rosette.

Although they should not be regarded with the seriousness and devotion of a show dog owner who has qualified for Cruft's, rather as a pleasant country occasion whereby club funds will also benefit, the fact remains that some dogs of a working type are kept by a few people purely for showing at these events. This is certainly not why the shows were developed and, if you are to get full enjoyment from attending these gatherings, you must bear this in mind. It is more important to show that you are a caring owner than it is for the world to see that you are in possession of the best terrier. Generally, however, the two go hand in hand and a well-kept animal has more chance of being shown than one which is kept in the dark recesses of the owner's shed and never sees anyone unless it is working.

## HOW THE SHOWS ARE RUN

Originally, it was impossible to enter your terrier for a working show unless you held a Working Certificate signed by the local Master of foxhounds saying that your dog had gone to ground in his presence at a meet of his hounds. There are, I believe, still some shows where a class for terriers with these certificates is included but, although I have been to many, I cannot recall a schedule in which this class appeared.

It is obviously impossible to organise such an event under Kennel Club rules as the entrants are not generally pedigree stock. There is, however, no doubt that the Jack Russell type will eventually be recognised as a breed by the Kennel Club because of the animal's popularity and the extra revenue that its inclusion would generate. It is to be hoped that when this does happen, it will not result in the working and show stock becoming two completely separate types. Parson Jack Russell once made a remark when discussing another breed of terriers which had just received Kennel Club status in his time: 'True terriers they were, but differing from the present show dogs as the wild eglantine differs from a garden rose.'

At the moment, show organisers generally include between ten and a dozen classes which cater for all the varieties, such as Border, Lakeland and Jack Russell types both smooth and rough. There are classes for dogs and bitches within these breeds, classes for puppies under six months, for young dogs or bitches between six months and a year, veterans over eight years and several other local

Terrier shows should be seen as a day out rather then being taken seriously.

'specialities' all culminating in a championship cup for the best terrier. In some cases, a cup for the best dog and bitch with smaller ones being given as prizes for the winners of individual classes are also awarded, but it is more usual for the winners to receive a rosette and a small medallion. The larger, championship cups are always perpetual with the winners only retaining the cup for a period of twelve months.

Unlike the larger Kennel Club shows where it is necessary to enter the relevant classes some weeks in advance, entry to the terrier shows run by hunts, agricultural societies and clubs, can be made on the day, usually to the secretary who will be found in a small tent or the back of a horse trailer. If you are unsure as to which class to enter, ask the secretary who will be able to advise. It may even be possible to enter one dog in more than one class. It depends to some extent upon the size of the show as to how many rings will be used but even the smallest affairs have two show rings in order to get through the entries more quickly.

Some organisations may also be running an 'exemption' dog show for breeds other than terriers and so you should acquaint yourself with which ring is going to be used for your particular class. It also pays to remain somewhere near the ring (the beer tent is as good a place as any!) as even though you may have watched a couple of classes in progress and worked out an approximate time for your own class, if the class prior to yours is poorly subscribed, it may be over in five minutes and you will miss the call to entrants. The stewards will endeavour to see that all competitors are in the ring before allowing the judge to continue – even to the extent of calling out any missing numbers over the public address system – but they cannot be expected to wait until you have rushed back to the car for your terrier, put on the number given to you by the secretary when you paid the entry fee and dragged the dog into the show ring.

## JUDGES AND WHAT THEY LOOK FOR

There can be either one or two judges in each ring and they will have been asked to judge by the organisers because of their knowledge and reputation concerning terriers. It is unlikely that they will be paid anything apart from perhaps travelling expenses. They are usually ordinary working people who, to judge at a weekend show, may have had to leave immediately after arriving home from work in order to travel a long distance to the show. They may be lucky and be offered a bed by one of the organisers or may have to be booked into a pub or guest house. Either way, they are spending a good deal of time away from home and their family.

For all this effort and inconvenience, they are more likely to receive abuse rather than praise, as in any class there can only be one person who feels that the judge knows his job, and that is the eventual winner. All the rest, especially those whose dogs may have won at a show the week before under another judge, will leave the ring somewhat disgruntled. Do not fall into this trap: remember this chapter's opening paragraph and that the whole business of working terrier shows is purely and simply, a matter for fun, enjoyment and meeting new people.

The judges will, however, take their job as seriously as possible and will be looking for a dog which they would wish to take home. They will keep at the back of their minds the fact that the hunt's

terrier man has paid exactly the same entrance fee as the little boy with his pet on a string or the old woman from down the road and judge their animals with exactly the same care and attention.

The points for which they are looking are the same as you would bear in mind when choosing a pup or a young, untried terrier which you have been lucky enough to find for sale. (As an aside to this, never buy a terrier which has been entered: it cannot be much good or else the vendor would not wish to sell.) An overall, 'game' appearance is essential and will undoubtedly catch the judges' eyes. Straight legs at the correct length; a deep chest with plenty of heart and lung room and a good square, strong-looking head are all essential pointers for which the judges will be looking before they eventually decide which way the rosettes should be awarded.

## IN THE RING

Once the stewards have called out the class number, the competitor should make his way into the ring and join the line-up on the opposite side to where the judges are standing. When everyone who has entered the particular class is present, the steward will indicate that the line should begin to walk around the perimeter ropes and this will give the judge an opportunity to pick out one or two animals which he particularly likes. The line will, after a short time, be halted and the judge will go to each owner and terrier in order to take a closer look at the individual dog. The teeth, jaws, feet and chest width will all be considered and, as mentioned earlier, each terrier will receive equal attention.

Judging is not always an easy matter.

'Straight legs and a deep chest.'

After a close inspection, each owner will be asked to walk his dog away and then back to the judges, which will give them an opportunity to see how the dog moves. Finally, the line will be asked to move around once more and it is then that the judges will make their eventual decision. The lucky owners will be asked to come towards the centre of the ring by the steward but if you are fortunate enough to be the first pulled forward do not immediately assume that you are in line for first prize as, if several dogs are of the highest quality, the judges may pull out as many as six animals for closer inspection. Even if there are four rosettes rather than the more usual first, second and third, two out of the six are bound to be disappointed and will hear the words 'Thank you, ladies and gentlemen', indicating that their chance has gone.

The rosettes are given out by the steward who will take your name and entry number. Those who have come first in a particular class, will have to hang around until the end of the show so that they can be included in the championship class, in which all the winners, no matter what their breed, are brought together for the judges to choose the 'Best in Show'.

## SHOWING THE TERRIER

One of the first pieces of advice which should be given to the potential show entrant is to allow your dog time to empty himself before going into the show ring. There can be nothing more embarrassing for the owner than to have to stand and wait as his terrier cocks his leg against one of the ring posts or squats, thereby halting the line which is walking around in front of the judges. If travelling to the show has meant covering a fair distance, or even if it hasn't but you have not had time to let the dog out for a long run at home, it is important to make sure that the terrier on show is given a few minutes in the car park.

There are several other points which the owner should consider upon entering the show ring. First and foremost, keep the dog on a short lead and stand as far away as possible from the next competitor. It is well known that terriers of any breed can be highly volatile and the excitement generated when several dogs are in close proximity is often sufficient to set off a full-scale fight. For this reason, you should never tie a dog near the show ring and leave it unattended as its inevitable yapping will be seen as competition by those terriers under the judge. It will, literally, cause their hackles to rise.

There should be no need to 'pose' your dog as is so often seen at the more serious shows such as Cruft's. Tails do not need to be held or the legs tapped forward into a correct showing position. What is important, however, is that the dog should be used to being handled by the judge, who may wish to use the tail in order to lift up the hind quarters and assess the potential strength which is so necessary in a working terrier. It is better to tell him that your dog is not to be trusted before he takes hold of the tail or attempts to examine the teeth for signs of an undershot or overshot jaw, rather than let him find out for himself.

You will not be penalised for bringing in such a dog if fair warning is given, as the judge can use his experience and expertise to check out the dog visually rather than physically. However, if you intend to do a lot of showing with a particular terrier, it will certainly pay to spend time at home in getting the dog accustomed to being handled by strangers. At first, you should do all the handling and test for any areas on the body which the dog is not too keen on you touching. As the dog relaxes, members of the family can be brought in to pick up the dog, 'span' him and open the mouth until it is possible to persuade a friend who is, nevertheless, a stranger to the terrier, to move around the dog as a judge would.

Whilst preparing for the show ground at home, it will prove to be beneficial in encouraging the dog to stand correctly and with an alert expression, if you make judicious use of biscuits held in the hand. This method of getting the dog's initial interest is well known amongst hunts and their huntsmen who use the biscuit to persuade hounds to stand correctly at their shows. At first, show the titbit to the terrier and then throw it, allowing the dog to follow up and eat it. Repeat this several times until the animal is watching the hand which throws the biscuits. As you enter the ring, give a piece to the dog who will then continue to look at the hands in the hope of receiving more offerings.

One final, possibly obvious, point is to put the terrier between yourself and the judges. It is no use expecting them to be able to assess the dog's potential if it is hidden for most of the time behind the legs of the handler.

## PREPARATION FOR THE SHOW

With a healthy and well-kept terrier there is likely to be very little preparation necessary prior to the show. Bathing the

Spanning a terrier. The average person's hands should just be able to meet around the rib-cage.

dog frequently will only result in some of the hair's natural oils and protective greases being removed, which is bound to be detrimental to the animal when working.

If, for one reason or another, it is felt necessary to bath the dog, try to obtain a shampoo recommended by the vet, which will also act as an ectoparasital treatment, killing off fleas, lice, ticks and mange. Keep the animal reasonably warm and, apart from patting off the worst of the excess water with a towel, allow the terrier to dry out naturally. This will cause the least amount of damage to the protective guard hairs of the coat.

Dogs with a high proportion of white in their coats are usually made even whiter by a dusting of chalk when the animal concerned is being shown at a Kennel Club event, but this degree of preparation is certainly not necessary for the working terrier enthusiast. Indeed it has been known for a Jack Russell type terrier, which was supposed to be nearly all white but was more of a sandy colour due to it being on the ground in the morning, to carry off the cup for the 'Best Terrier in Show'. Despite the obvious discoloration, it possessed all the other necessary qualifications.

This dual role of working and showing a terrier all in one day is not, however, to be recommended, especially if it is done in the fond belief that a little dirt will impress the judges and lead them into giving first prize because the dog is so obviously a worker. One judge to whom I talked, expressed a personal opinion that a dog which is to be entered in a show on the Sunday afternoon

If you intend to show your terrier, a piece of biscuit undoubtedly
helps to attract his attention and. . .

. . .very soon, he will begin to stand to his best advantage.

should not be worked on the preceding Saturday let alone on the morning of the show.

It should be possible to brush out any dust and dirt in the coat rather than indulge in continuous washing. To make this job even easier, especially with a rough or broken-coated dog, it may not be a bad idea to strip out the coat. Although usually associated with the show bench, the stripping out of the worst of a rough coat will help with brushing and general cleanliness of a working terrier. It might be thought that by trimming out the outer guard hairs, you will also lose much of the essential oils, but it is not the length of the coat which counts, more its density. Strip-

ping a rough-coated dog only results in shortening the guard hairs rather than removing them.

The removal of the worst of the outer hair also makes it easier to spot potential troubles. Wounds are the most obvious examples but you need to be constantly aware of the possibility of fleas or ticks. The latter are usually found around the head area, especially the ears and neck – areas which, without stripping, could easily be neglected. At a time when almost everyone smoked, the usual procedure for the removal of ticks was to apply a lighted cigarette to the head of the parasite. As the head is almost always buried in the animal's skin, the nearest you can get is the blood-

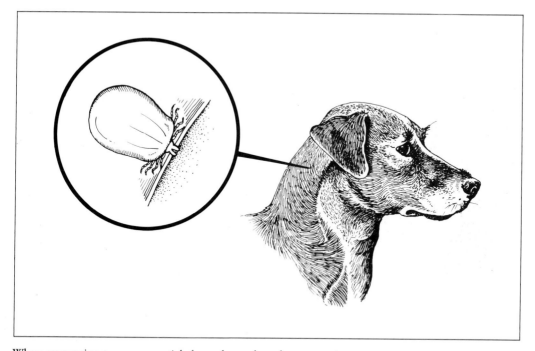

When attempting to remove a tick from the neck and ear area, it is all too easy to destroy the blood-engorged body and yet leave the head firmly encased in the skin. If this is left unnoticed, it could cause some very bad sores. It is, therefore, important to ensure that the whole tick is removed.

engorged body. Whilst the application of a cigarette certainly makes the tick shrink and appear to drop off, the head will undoubtedly be left in place causing bad sores. A better procedure is to dab the tick with either petrol or paraffin and then seize it with a pair of tweezers, jerking it off with a quick twist.

Provided that you know exactly how to do it, the stripping or plucking out of any surplus hair can be done by hand. Some terriers, due to their individual metabolism, produce softer hair than others, and despite the twice-yearly moult during which the winter hairs are replaced by the shorter and finer ones of summer, which are in turn superseded by the thicker, warmer type to give protection from the winter cold, nature often neglects to pass on the message. The result is that large areas of matted hair

remains on the body and this misalliance of natural functions leaves the animal looking bulkier and hairier than it should. Left alone this dead hair will continue to matt and the increase of oils will leave the animal with an unpleasant smell. In this situation you should either pluck out these areas of hair by hand or with the aid of a stripping knife which can be bought from a pet shop.

## TERRIER RACING

Most organisers of terrier shows also attempt to set up a few terrier racing heats to finish off the day's events. These cannot, by any stretch of the imagination, be taken seriously and it is simply an amusing spectacle for both competitors and onlookers.

The start of a terrier race. Some entrants seem to be unsure as to their exact purpose in life!

The track is marked out by means of a rope or line of straw bales. Its length very often depends on where the event is being held but as a general guide, it is possibly a distance of around fifty metres. At one end is a block of traps, similar to those found at a greyhound stadium, which can hold four or six terriers individually. At the other end of the track is a winding mechanism, geared by means of cogs so that the bottom axle or spindle is going at twice as many revolutions as the hand-held turning piece at the top. Very often, it will be noticed that the contraption has been made from an old bicycle frame. I have also seen a more basic idea where a Land Rover's back wheel is used. A wire or rope, the same length as the course over which the terriers have to run, is then fixed to the winding mechanism. At the end closest to the trap is attached a fox's brush or clump or rag which, once the terriers have been placed in the trap, is then used to tease them through the meshed fronts. By this time, there is a great deal of noise, not only from the terriers – who very quickly get excited – but also from the owners themselves! The trap doors are then simultaneously lifted, the person in charge of winding begins to crank away and they are off!

Sometimes, when the dogs are particularly well matched it can be quite a difficult matter assessing just which dog has in fact won, but there are usually sufficient spectators around the winning line to clarify any doubts. It is advisable to have someone whom the dog knows waiting at the winning post in order to pick up the terrier before he begins to attack the quarry or his fellow competitors. Some terriers complete about half the course and then dive off into the crowd looking for a dog with which to start a scrap. Others amble out of the traps not quite sure of what is going on and look incredulously at the fast-departing fox's brush before giving themselves a shake and wandering back to their owner.

With the excitement, it is quite likely that your dog, should you choose to enter him in such an event, will start fighting but, provided that you are positioned close enough to intervene, there is no real worry if the two dogs are making a lot of noise. It is only when they go quiet that you need really have cause for concern as this generally means that they have got hold of each other. At least two people will be needed to separate the dogs and I have seen one person pick up his dog by the back legs, tail or whatever part of the anatomy is readily available and lift both dogs off the ground. Even then, they will not let go and it usually requires one person to hold one terrier by the tail and the scruff of his neck whilst the other chokes the second animal off either by squeezing his windpipe, or by putting his hands around the dog's throat at the same time as pushing the biter's tongue upwards with his thumbs. Be sure to keep your hands at the scruff of the neck or at least out of biting distance when the two dogs have eventually been separated, otherwise they will latch on to anything literally 'at hand' in their excited state.

I have, on one occasion, seen a terrier race set up in the manner of the Grand National by having specially constructed brushwood fences situated at strategic intervals across the course. Obviously these were only as high as a terrier could comfortably be expected to jump and had gaps running down the middle through which the fox's brush was propelled. It was quite an amusing sight to

When two terriers fight, it usually requires two pairs of hands to separate them. The biter grips so tightly that it is possible to pick up both animals by holding the tail of the one which is being bitten. One way of separating the two is for one pair of hands to hold the bitten terrier by the scruff of the neck whilst the other tries to prise the biter's jaws apart. An alternative to this would be to grip the biter's windpipe and choke it off.

see the terriers jump over the fences, stop momentarily in order to look around and then, upon spying the 'quarry', engage top gear and dash off in hot pursuit. It would, I suppose, be a simple matter for anyone thinking of laying out a course on similar lines, to use straw bales as fences rather than going to the trouble of making proper hurdles.

## A QUESTION OF HEALTH

It is vitally important that you have your terrier properly inoculated as a puppy and then ensure that he is given 'booster' injections at the appropriate times. Some owners neglect to do this, feeling that it is unnecessary expense when their terrier is never likely to come into contact with any other dogs. This is, in my opinion, a very narrow-minded attitude and no dog should be taken where others are to be found if he has not been inoculated – this includes terrier shows. I would like to see a nationwide rule stating that owners may not even take a dog out of the car before going to the entry tent and showing the secretary an up-to-date vaccination certificate. This could even be shown to the person taking money at the car park entrance if it was felt that the show secretary would not have time to deal with both checking certificates and organising the entry forms.

It should go without saying that, if your dog appears to be under the weather on the morning of the show, attending with it is out of the question unless you have been given the all-clear by a veterinary surgeon. Even then, entering a class is likely to be a waste of time as, like humans, a dog which feels ill is not going to show himself to his best advantage.

If a dog enters the car quite happily but, upon arrival at the show, looks a little sorry for himself, it may just be that he is suffering from travel-sickness and should improve after being walked around the car park for a few minutes. It is possible to purchase travel sickness tablets from the vet but it will pay, first of all, to try the following. If the terrier is normally transported in the rear of the vehicle, put him between the passenger's legs in the front where he cannot see anything and, because of the confined space, is kept quiet and secure. In some makes of car, the back end slides about on the road and it is often this action which causes the sickness.

# CAR TRAVELLING

It is almost an impossibility to stop a terrier from leaping from seat to seat or even passenger to passenger if it is given the freedom of the vehicle. Their favourite stance seems to be with their hind legs on the front passenger's seat, front paws on the dashboard and nose pressed up to the window or, in some cases, the air vent. In this position they are then ready for anything and if a dog or other interesting object is seeen along the roadside they will leap from front to back in a frenzy of excitement. This is, of course an extremely dangerous practice and so, if you intend to do a great deal of showing and therefore a great deal of travelling, the best solution is to make a travelling box. This need not be very elaborate. A tea chest turned on its side with a piece of weld mesh cut to the correct size and hinged by means of a couple of fencing staples is all that is required for one dog.

As mentioned on page 94, you should never let two or more dogs travel together as it is possible that a fight may ensue and, in the middle of a traffic jam, the driver will not be able to do anything about it. A partitioned travelling box can be made very cheaply out of plywood. If the car is an estate type, the ends and partition should be cut at the same angle as the tailgate when it is closed. Any battening on to which you will screw the back, roof, floor and hinged front can be nailed on to the outside of these ends rather than the more usual practice of fixing it inside. This will prevent any injuries to the occupants and make the boxes easier to clean. The front or door section must hinge upwards otherwise the terriers' feet and legs may get damaged as they

A travelling box. Looking closely at the interior base, it can be seen that there is a groove along which a thin partition can slide to divide the box when two terriers are being carried.

jump into the box. The addition of a narrow piece of plywood along the bottom will stop any bedding from being pulled out as well as giving somewhere to fix a couple of fastening bolts.

Newspapers, a piece of carpet or a clean hessian sack are all that is required as a floor covering but it is important that some type of material is used in order to prevent the terriers from sliding around on the smooth plywood base.

# 6  Kennel Talk

There are two very differing opinions which become evident whenever the question of kennelling is raised amongst a group of terrier owners. The majority feeling seems to be that a working dog kept in the house is likely to be too 'soft' to be of any use as a sporting companion and is also likely to develop bad habits. This latter accusation applies more when the working dog in question is one of the gundog breeds for, with highly-trained dogs such as these, it is all too easy for members of the family to unwittingly ruin an animal through lax discipline. Telling a spaniel to 'hup' and not bothering to make sure that the command is carried out, brings it a stage closer to 'running-in' when on the shooting field. Letting a labrador carry a child's doll around the house and then, because no one is around to take the 'retrieve' begin to chew it, is asking for a dog to become hard-mouthed.

Obviously, the terrier is not as highly trained as the above breeds, nor does it need to be. So surely there can be no real reason why a working terrier cannot be a family pet, provided that it is adequately supervised and not allowed out to hunt on its own. By doing so, in the opinion of the second half of the group, the dog will understand the owner better by being in constant contact. Where several terriers are kept or when a pup is entering an establishment in which there are other dogs kennelled outside, there may well be no alternative but to use an outbuilding and run.

With puppies, however, it is important not to keep them in the kennel for long periods during their first few formative months as, due to a lack of necessary mental stimulation, they will be much slower to mature than would one which has access to continual human contact. Conversely, if the pup is given too much freedom there may eventually come a time when he gives the owner a complete lack of response, a problem which hardly ever occurs with a kennel-kept dog. Each time the kennel-kept terrier is taken out, his attention will be on the owner and, perhaps more importantly, the owner's attention will be on the dog, thereby ensuring that he gets away with nothing.

House dog or kennel dog? The choice is yours and each has its advantages and disadvantages.

## POSITIONING THE KENNEL

Fortunately, the terrier needs very little room and so almost any small, unused area of the garden can be the location for a kennel. The place chosen must comply with certain rules, however, if the dog is to remain healthy and alert.

Provided that they are not allowed to lay in front of the fire one minute and the next being put into a kennel experiencing sub-zero temperatures, dogs can endure almost any degree of cold, if it is not accompanied by draughts. It is therefore essential that the kennel area be protected from wind which will find its way through cracks in the door or leave the terrier facing a wind-tunnel effect every time it enters its run. If there is no alternative location, a kennel which has to be built in an exposed area could be protected by the addition of baffle-boarding or a sheet of corrugated tin around the base. If it is felt necessary to carry out this operation, make sure that the inclusion of some form of wind protection is not to the exclusion of another important factor, namely that the dog's view of its immediate environment is not obscured.

This is another point to bear in mind when deciding upon the ideal kennel location as, just like humans, dogs of any breed will very soon become bored if there is nothing to look at. It may only be someone hanging out the washing or the daily arrival of the postman but at least there will be periods in the terrier's day when it will have something or someone on which to focus its attention. Dogs, but especially terriers with their high metabolism, need some diversion in their kennel life if they are not to develop habits such as chewing the woodwork or pacing up and down. This could lead to anxiety problems similar to these found in some zoo animals, which, in turn, will eventually result in a loss of condition.

Although kennel dogs need to see activity, terriers should not be able to see each other so take care when locating more than one kennel that the runs are not directly opposite each other (across a yard for instance). If this positioning is inevitable build some form of screen as, if you neglect this, the constant pacing or running from one side of the run to the other, sometimes with the addition of a bounce against the wall, as if the terrier is trying to climb it, will once again result in a mentally maladjusted dog and a loss of condition. Why terriers should be more prone to this type of hyperactivity is not really understood but it is a problem realised by almost all experienced terrier owners.

You must also make sure that when two or more kennels are being situated in close proximity to each other, there is adequate screening protection between the different dogs. It has been known for a terrier to have to be destroyed due to the fact that the dividing partition was only half-boarded and his leg slipped between the partition and became trapped. The neighbouring terrier then ripped the animal's leg and foot so badly that there was no alternative but to have the unfortunate dog put down.

Yet another important question when choosing the ideal site for the kennel is how much sun it will get. Too much sun brings the danger of both kennel and run turning into an oven during the hottest of weather; too little leaves the possibility that the dog will be missing out on some of the advantageous vitamins available from the sun's rays. The problem of too much sun can be overcome to some extent by the addition of a tarpaulin sheet fixed over the top of a run. Another answer would be to include a bench in the run area at a height suitable to give the terrier the option of sleeping either on top or underneath where it will obviously be a few degrees cooler in the heat of the day.

The kennel and run should also be placed as far away as possible from any neighbours if you wish to avoid any bad feeling which may arise as a result of constant yapping from your dog. I know of several terrier owners living in built-up areas who only use the kennel

Many terrier owners use a run and small sleeping box during the daytime but kennel them in confined boxes at night.

Confining terriers in small boxes within an enclosed shed will help to prevent midnight disturbance if you live in a heavily populated area. Newspapers provide an easily disposable bedding.

and run during the day, bringing the dog into an enclosed shed sectioned off into small cubicles at night. By doing so, the terriers are unable to see the neighbour's cat crossing the garden and are less likely to hear it, preventing the need for the owners to turn out in the middle of the night in order to quieten their animals.

Mrs Anne Brewer of the 'Tarsia' kennels takes this idea one stage further even though she lives well out in the Hampshire countryside. During the day her terriers are kept in spacious runs in one corner of which is a small sleeping box, and they are then taken into quarters which are heated in the worst of winter weather. The inside of these quarters is then divided into small sleeping areas as shown here. In using this arrangement, Mrs Brewer feels that she is gaining many advantages over those owners who keep their dogs kennelled all the time. Firstly, the terriers are constantly being handled, making them easier to show. Secondly, by keeping the dogs in pairs during the day, they are creating an interest in each other, but when it comes to sleeping, and the terriers are 'put to bed' separately, there is no danger that one dog will prevent the other from getting into the sleeping quarters as would be the case if kept kennelled in the more orthodox way. Cleaning out either sleeping quarters or daytime runs is made easier by the fact that it can be done when the dogs are elsewhere.

Drainage is also important and the inevitable water from cleaning out should be able to run off and soak away at a fair distance from the kennel area. If this problem is not given adequate thought at the planning stage, the front of the kennels where dogs and humans walk will soon become an unpleasant quagmire looking more like a First World War battlefield than someone's carefully tended garden.

Local authority planning permission will not be required before building a kennel provided that certain conditions are met. These are:

1. That the building is for the benefit of the house and is connected with its residential use. (Buildings to house animals kept for the domestic needs or personal enjoyment of the occupants of the house are included in this category. It must, therefore, be assumed that planning permission would be required if you were intending to run a boarding kennels from the premises.)
2. No part of the building or structure projects beyond the forwardmost part of any wall of the original house which faces a highway (a public footpath may count as a highway).
3. That the height of the building is

not more than four metres, if it has a ridged roof, or three metres otherwise; and
4. The addition of the structure will not result in more than half the garden of the house being covered by buildings.

## KENNEL CONSTRUCTION

I have tried to point out in the relevant places the need to realise that terriers are different from other breeds of dogs, and nowhere is this more important than when discussing kennel construction.

You should never kennel more than two terriers together and, if you do decide to keep both sexes, it is often the best idea to kennel a male and female together. Care will obviously have to be taken at the approximate time the bitch is expected to come into season and alternative accommodation found for the three-week 'danger' period. The characters of the individual animals must be well known by the owner in order to kennel them together safely and even then it is not unknown for mother and son who have been together since birth to suddenly take a dislike to each other.

The actual design of the kennel will of course depend on where it is being situated but some general points apply no matter what type of construction is being built. Perhaps the best arrangement is for an area of approximately two metres by four metres to be used to include both run and sleeping quarters. A box of around one metre square is ample sleeping space for two terriers but there is no reason why a larger, traditional-looking dog kennel should not be incorporated into the run area. The one illustrated has an advantage

The traditional type of dog kennel can prove to be a useful home for a single terrier. This one has an obvious hinged roof for easy cleaning. Only use such a kennel within a confined run and *never* tie a dog to the kennel.

over the more basic forms as, if you look closely, you will see that the whole of the roof area is hinged and capable of being lifted to facilitate easy cleaning.

Never be tempted into using a kennel of this nature in a situation where it is necessary to tie the dog to it by means of a rope or chain, as I have seen two terriers hanged in just such a way. On both occasions, the terriers jumped on to the roof and slipped down the opposite side leaving them suspended in mid-air. By the time the respective owners went out to feed or exercise their dogs, it was too late and they had been choked to death by their collars.

The size and height from the ground of the sleeping boxes is quite important as terriers seem to take great delight in fouling their beds. If the box is too large they will do whatever they have to do in there rather than take the trouble to come outside. If the entrance hole is at the right height, a male dog will cock his leg and urinate from the outside causing the inside to become wet and smelly. It is, however, important that the box is raised off the ground in order to prevent a draught reaching the inhabitants. Once again, some form of baffle board at the base of the entrance will help to prevent both draughts and the undesirable habits of a male terrier!

Concrete is the best form of flooring for the run as, although shingle can be used, it is very difficult to keep clean and cannot be regularly disinfected in the same way that concrete can. Likewise, even a large grassed run will soon become muddy with the constant use and is the ideal home for certain worms and parasites. When the concrete is laid, ensure that it is of a thick enough depth to prevent it becoming cracked and flaky in frosty weather. Every schoolboy knows that water which turns to ice is strong enough to crack a boulder as it expands and the same principle will be at work on a kennel floor, due to the fact that it will require frequent washing. Also make sure that there is a sufficient slope on the run to take away the worst of any water and that it will run off in the direction where it is least likely to form a muddy mess. If you use sleeping boxes of the type advocated, then their floors will obviously be made of wood, but if you decide to have a larger kennel at one end of a run, the floor of this can also be made of concrete and a sleeping bench constructed above. Unlike the bench in the run which I mentioned earlier, this one should not allow the terrier access to the underneath as it may be found that the dog takes to sleeping

97

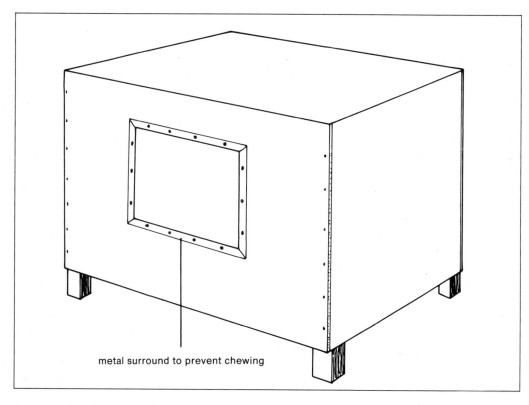

metal surround to prevent chewing

A sleeping box for terriers should be of small dimensions if you wish to prevent the occupant from fouling his bed or lying in a draught. A metal surround fitted to the opening stops any unwanted chewing by the inhabitants.

under, rather than on top of the bench and the whole point of making a warm draught-proof bed is defeated.

The run part is best made in sections and when put into position on the concrete should be fixed in a way which allows a small. gap between the bottom of the section and the concrete base. Water can then be brushed away via this gap and the section itself is likely to last several years longer than it would if continually soaking up the moisture from the floor. Provided that the bed is warm and dry, there is no real reason to include any boarding along the bottom part of the sections but most kennel designs include this feature. Ideally, the frame of the section should be fitted with weld mesh but this is, unfortunately, very expensive. If it can possibly be afforded, then use this material in preference to any other. If not, you will have to resort to a material such as chain link which is trickier to fix but is much cheaper. Chain link should be a sufficient deterrent for all but the most determined escapologist but it must be said that I have known a whippet to chew through chain link in a very short space of time. For this reason, wire netting, even the strongest gauge, is useless in kennel construction.

If an individual terrier has a propensity for chewing, the parts of the woodwork which he seems to favour (usually the edges of his box or bed or perhaps the bottom of the doors) could be protected by bending and fitting some thin metal strips over them. A good wood preserver should be used to protect the framework of the sections, and you will find that this operation is more easily carried out during the actual construction and before the wire is fitted. Despite its relative cheapness, do not be tempted into using creosote for this job. It is not an effective form of protector, it fades quickly, never seems to totally dry

An adequate overhang will prevent heavy rain from entering the kennel and run but will still allow patches of sunshine in which the inhabitants can sun themselves.

out and, unless you are prepared to wait for a period of time before housing a dog in a bed and run thus treated, will prove detrimental to the animal's health.

Most terrier owners whom I have visited, seem to favour a covered-in roof section and, if you choose the smaller type of sleeping box, this is certainly a good idea as the dog will spend most of the day in the run. The possible problems of continuous rain and heat exhaustion from an unshaded kennel and run are immediately eradicated but the terrier will still be able to find a sunny corner in which to sunbathe as, at certain times of the day, the sun is bound to enter via the sides.

If it is decided to include an overall roof, it is not a bad idea to ensure that there is a fairly generous overhang at both the front and back which will stop the worst of the driving rain. When it runs off, the water should fall far enough away to prevent mud and water from splashing into the actual kennel area. Roofing material such as corrugated asbestos sheeting is ideal as it is longer lasting and cannot rust unlike corrugated iron sheeting. The point must be made that, although still known as asbestos, the modern sheeting does not actually contain the substance which made using the material so dangerous some years ago. It is possible to use perspex sheeting to cover the roof. This is initially much cheaper than any other alternatives but because of its lightness, it will soon be cracked or broken by the inevitable strong winds and will need almost continual replacing, with new sheets adding to the initial cost. Another disadvantage is that after a few years the sun's ultraviolet rays have an adverse effect on the chemical properties within the sheet, causing it to become opaque

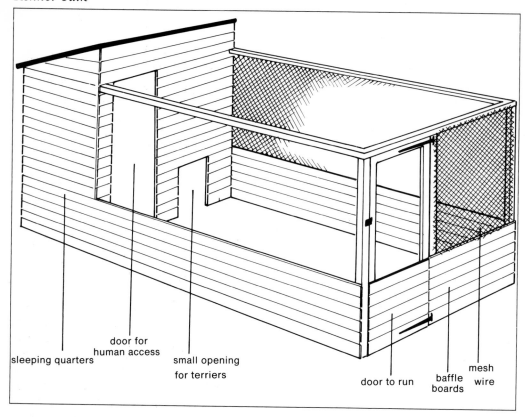

A commonly-used design of kennel and run. As can be seen from the text, this arrangement is not necessarily ideal housing for terriers.

and brittle. I have been told that this problem has now been overcome by the manufacturers but if I were constructing new kennels, I would still prefer to use sheets of the asbestos type.

If it is decided to use an open-topped run then, depending on the height of the side sections, and the agility of your dog, it may be necessary to cover the top in order to prevent his escape. There are two ways to do this: you can either close it in completely with wire netting, which although unsuitable for use in the side sections is ideal for this job; or fix battens of around half a metre in length to the top of the sections, facing inwards. Several strands of galvanised

wire, fitted closely together in the manner of barbed wire around a prisoner-of-war camp, will prevent the terrier from being able to clamber up the inside and hoist itself over the top.

## FEEDING: NATURALLY OR FOR CONVENIENCE?

There is no doubt that feeding raw flesh offers vital nutrients and dogs which are fed by such methods seem to suffer less in the way of disorders.

Unpleasant though the feeding of flesh and offal may at first seem, it pays to remember that the dogs are, relatively speaking, still very close to nature in their pack and feeding habits. Huskies are a good example and although domesticated still retain a fair proportion of their natural metabolism – so much so that many interested modern-day breeders have found it beneficial to feed their dogs raw rabbit still 'in the skin' so that they can obtain the necessary roughage. I am not for one moment suggesting that you should feed your terrier raw rabbit meat as, along with chicken bones, there is always the danger that small bones can splinter and become stuck in the dog's throat, causing death by choking.

Two or three decades ago, it was found that some herding dogs in Northumbria were beginning to suffer from an ailment known as 'Black Tongue', the cause of which was at first unknown but eventually it was realised that the problem arose at exactly the same period as rabbits began to suffer from the first ever bout of myxomatosis. At the time, it was common practice for shepherds and farmers to feed their animals nothing but flaked maize. The dogs had, however, been augmenting this rather meagre diet with rabbits caught during the course of their work and these had given them the necessary proteins and vitamins to remain healthy and hard-working. The absence of rabbits destroyed this balance between meat and cereal and, as a result, the dogs became ill.

Green tripe and paunch is rather revolting from the human point of view but, to dogs, it makes the ideal meal and is readily taken on board. In the wild, lions will rip out and eat the stomachs of their quarry before moving on to the red meat. Both tripe and paunch are full of low protein and can be given throughout a dog's life. Because of the protein factor, however, it should ideally be mixed with cereals such as flaked maize, rolled oats and rolled wheat. Even then, the mix is still not quite sufficient for a working dog and requires the addition of *sterilised* bonemeal (not the kind used by gardeners!). Ox tripe contains more suet and so will not require the addition of as much cereal. Red meat is a useful and healthy food but, in the opinion of most vets and experienced dog owners, should not be given continually without a break as it is thought to have a toxic effect upon the dog's kidney.

It is usually only in hunting establishments that the feeding of raw flesh is carried out and the majority give their hounds a break from red meat at least once a week, substituting either a cereal porridge or paunches from casualties collected that week from the local farmers. Others starve their hounds for one day a week, feeling that it gives the digestive system an all-important rest. This is, once again, not too far removed from the way in which dogs would have behaved in the wild as it is unlikely that they would have been successful in killing every day.

The way in which raw meat is given varies from hunt to hunt, some merely skinning a carcass and letting the hounds rip the meat from the bones, others cutting off slices of meat and using the bones as a stock for the cereal porridge. One terrier owner to whom I talked believes that the latter method should be taken a stage further and the strips of meat minced as, because of the pack instinct, the dog has got to eat quickly. Having been minced, the food can then be gulped down at a rapid rate. Whether this is really necessary to the owner with only a couple of terriers is open to doubt

Not many terrier owners feed raw flesh these days and it is usually only in hunting establishments where this is still carried out.

but it is nevertheless an interesting school of thought.

In fact, if you only own a couple of terriers, the trouble involved in getting hold of farm casualties, skinning and jointing them for the freezer and then finding a way of getting rid of the skin and bones, is not likely to be worth while. It will be easier for those terrier people involved in some way with the local hunt as there is usually enough meat and offal there to be able to give a little away to interested parties.

Green tripe is readily available frozen from most pet suppliers and comes quite cheaply in pre-packed blocks which can be kept in the household freezer. It does, however, have one minor disadvantage. Once it has de-frosted it smells revolting and what is more, the dog will soon begin to smell the same way. This may not be too much of a problem with a dog which is kennelled outside but is not too pleasant a prospect when keeping a house dog! If you decide to feed your

terrier on meat and offal, it should be remembered that though generally more beneficial than tins of processed meat and expensive biscuit, the diet is likely to cause more problems with worms than you would normally expect. There are at least five species of the tapeworm genus which occur in the small intestines, all of which are more likely to present themselves in an environment where only raw meat is fed. The intestines of a terrier fed entirely on meat could contain up to 74 per cent more tapeworms than one which is fed on a proprietary type of food.

Because there is nowadays so much choice available, you should take a close look at some of the all-in-one foods before making a final decision as to the best way of feeding your terrier.

All are well balanced and nutritionally sound but their continuous use could cause problems if you do not take the trouble to find out exactly what the food contains.

I have tried several makes on my gundogs and terriers but have noticed that some cause scouring or are just not liked by the dogs. Those which make the dogs 'loose' are, I feel, too high in protein although it could merely be the fact that, in those which are supposed to be fed wet, the mixture has been made too sloppy. The type which I have now used daily for six years can be fed either wet or dry as it is basically biscuit and dried meat. My own dogs prefer it dry and will turn their noses up when we have scalded the biscuit in hot water in an effort to warm them up on a cold day. My assistant on the shoot feeds the same food to his spaniel and labrador but they prefer it wet and so it can only be assumed that wet or dry is an individual preference.

One example given to illustrate the importance of realising exactly what each food contains is copper retention. Known as Wilson's Disease in humans, it can kill a terrier if the feeding of a particular compound in which there exists too high a rate of copper is continued over a long period of time.

No dog should be kept without water for any period of time but when dry versions of the all-in-one type of feed are being given it is important that you keep a constant check on the water bowl as it has been noticed that a dog on this diet will consume a much greater volume of water than would normally be expected.

If only one dog is kept or several are kept singularly, marrow bones can prove to be a very beneficial addition to the animal's diet and will also help in keeping the terriers amused for the time when they are alone in the kennels. It is well

Feeding on dry meal.

It is important to supply plenty of fresh water when feeding a dry all-in-one type of meal.

known that chewing on a bone helps to keep gums and teeth healthy as well as clearing off the unwanted tartar.

## A DAILY ROUTINE

Every dog owner must, of necessity, have a daily routine. For the house dog there is very little to consider apart from exercise and a feeding time but the owners of kennelled terriers will, when the routine of kennel maintenance has to be fitted in around a job of work and there is no one else to share the chores, need to give day-to-day management some serious consideration.

In some people's opinions, real fitness can only be achieved by work but there is no doubt that regular exercising will help in attaining a reasonable degree of health and muscular improvement. This regime should commence with at least two daily outings. They need not be long periods of exercise – if the owner walks a mile then it is a pretty safe bet that his terriers will have run around for at least three or four. It is reckoned that sheep dogs working in moorland and similar open areas run fourteen miles to each one which the shepherd walks and on this basis, it would not be unreasonable to assume that an active terrier is capable of covering the distances mentioned above.

It would be logical to exercise morning and night, which will undoubtedly help in keeping the kennel clean, although cleanliness is likely to be determined by the time at which the terrier is fed. Most people have no option but to feed at night upon their return home but, despite a walk straight afterwards, it will take some hours for the food to be processed by the stomach and the dogs will have full bowels half-way through the night. If it is possible to persuade someone else to feed your animals at lunchtime and maybe even give them a quick run around the garden this will help, and the dogs' waste products will be evacuated during the evening exercise.

After the morning walk, the run should be swilled out with the contents of the water bowl and fresh water given. If a more thorough swilling out is required, the inclusion of a good quality disinfectant will remove any stains caused by faeces or urine. If you are dressed in work clothes, however, it may be advisable to leave this chore until evening as otherwise you will smell of the disinfectant all day. When more than one kennel has to be cleaned, a suit of nylon overtrousers and jacket may prove to be a useful investment. Tight sleeves, buttoned or elasticated at the wrist, will prevent any worries of unpleasant substances going up your arm!

Bedding can be changed on a weekly rather than a daily basis provided that it is not soiled, but the occupants will certainly appreciate the shaking up of whatever material is being used. By evening, they will have constructed a new little 'nest' in exactly the same place as it was in the morning, but a shaking up will at least have loosened any lumpiness and make the bed more likely to absorb any mud or moisture from the animal's coat. The great majority of dog owners use straw as bedding, and this is undeniably both warm and absorbent. It does, however, have the disadvantage of harbouring parasites. If straw is used, make sure that it is wheat and not barley as the husks and whiskers in the latter could cause problems by aggravating the inside of the terrier's ears. Oat straw tends to be brittle and is not as clean as the other two types so this should only be used if all attempts at getting hold of a bale or two of wheat straw have failed.

Wood shavings are an alternative and are readily available at most agricultural suppliers due to the fact that they are

Plenty of straw here! If it is decided to use straw as bedding, do not pick up the first available bale. If there is a choice, always use wheat.

becoming increasingly popular amongst the horse-owning fraternity. Try to pick out a bale which contains good quality white, flaky chips and definitely avoid the reddish variety which is obtained from softwoods and could cause skin irritations because of its highly resinous nature. Sawdust is not a good idea because the fine particles of dust may find their way into the terrier's eye. I have found that shredded newspaper (again easily obtainable because of its value as horse bedding) is the ideal answer. It is very absorbent and warm and any 'soiling' can be removed without necessitating a complete clear-out. Some suppliers of shredded paper add a viral disinfectant to their bales and this helps in the eternal war against parasites.

There are two minor disadvantages with both the shavings and the newspaper. Firstly because they are cut into flakes rather than strands, each time the dog jumps out of his box, he is bound to bring a small proportion of bedding with him, thereby making a mess of the kennel area. If, as recommended, this is swept out each morning, then there should not be too great a build up and they will not end up being blown around the garden or blocking up any drains. Secondly, there is the question of cost — you need to be prepared to pay around four times the price of straw for a bale of either shavings or paper.

Finally, although regular routine is advantageous in keeping terriers settled and content, there may be times when you have no alternative but to feed and exercise at irregular hours so that the dogs do not get a chance to use their efficient in-built 'clock'. As the time approaches for either food or a run, animals which have developed this timing will undoubtedly start to whine and yap as the all-important period in their day draws nearer. This noise will definitely not be appreciated by neighbours if you keep terriers in a relatively built-up area and, as it is vitally important for the working terrier owner to be seen in a favourable light by the general public, regular habits may have to go by the board rather than cause any bad feeling.

# 7 Health, Breeding and Puppy Care

Normally, terriers are extremely healthy animals and not susceptible to any serious problems. If it is intended to breed from your bitch it is vitally important to ensure that she is in a good condition and free from any ailments. Checking a terrier for any signs of being 'off colour' or possible diseases is, however, an all-year round occupation and, as such, should perhaps be discussed in general before going on to deal with the pregnant bitch in particular.

## DAY-TO-DAY HEALTH

### Worms

Terriers, like any other dogs, need worming occasionally and it is best to ask the vet for a suitable wormer rather than buy tablets over the pet shop counter. A broad-spectrum wormer will prove to be efficient in removing both tapeworm and roundworm.

Tapeworm is more readily found when uncooked meat is the main source of dietary income and the flesh of sheep has been found to contain more than its fair share of tapeworm inducing ingredients. Sometimes, the terrier is a host to 'whipworm' but once again a broad-spectrum wormer should prove an efficient form of eradication. The egg is, however, very long-lived and if a grass run is used, it will remain a potential source of infection for at least five years – another good reason why kennels and runs should be based on concrete.

The question of worms affecting humans should never be underestimated and both roundworm and hookworm can be a serious problem in this quarter. When man ingests the embryonated ova of any form of toxocara which has contaminated his fingers or food, hatching inevitably takes place and the larvae will invade the tissues of the body. Hookworm and tapeworm are very dangerous as, unlike most other parasites which cannot infect human tissue, they will affect the lungs and liver plus, in certain cases, the spleen, kidneys and bone marrow leaving a hydatid cyst for which at present the only feasible remedy is surgical removal.

Lungworm, although not common in dogs in Britain, is often first noticed by coughing, which some supposed experts put down to 'kennel cough'. In actual fact, from the veterinary point of view, 'kennel cough' is an ailment which may have several different causes, only one of which is worms found in the trachea and bronchi, particularly where these join together. Many cases are without symptoms but infection is sometimes characterised by a chronic dry cough, exacerbated by exercise, which occasionally ends with a retching action.

The potential danger of worms can be lessened by basing both kennel and run on concrete.

Particularly when a terrier is kept in a house, I have often heard it said, upon seeing the dog rubbing his bottom on the carpet, that he is suffering from worms but, in actual fact, this behaviour is more likely to be due to impaction or infection of the anal glands, which are needed by dogs in the wild to mark their territory. With domestication they have obviously outlived the use of these glands, and it is best to let the vet express them. Very occasionally it may be necessary to have them surgically removed.

Remaining at the unpleasant end of the dog, it is sometimes seen that the terrier appears to take great delight in consuming faeces, either his own or those of farm animals or wildlife. Unpleasant to the owner, it can be due to a diet deficiency. Depending on what food is being given as the day-to-day diet, it may pay to change over to fresh butcher's meat if you are feeding either

A dietary deficiency could be rectified by the daily addition of fresh meat. The skinning and storage of farm casualties is, however, not usually a practical proposition for the terrier owner with only one or two dogs in his kennel.

n all-in-one meal or the normal tinned meat and biscuit. Whatever is being fed; add a teaspoon of dried yeast to each eed.

## kin Irritations

The one thing to which terriers do seem usceptible is skin infections in their arious forms. You will sometimes notice your dog scratching his ears, vhich appear sore and inflamed. This ould be because of an infection lthough it is usually the longer-eared ariety of dogs which suffer from this, specially the spaniel breeds. The short ars of the terrier generally keep clean nd free from infection so it is more ikely that they have the relatively simple roblem of a lodged grass seed. This nay work its way out after two or three lays but if necessary, the vet can remove t under anaesthetic.

The opinion of a vet must obviously be acknowledged and adhered to and it is likely that Alugan will be prescribed for a general skin irritation. Occasionally, Quellada veterinary shampoo will be recommended and, of the many preparations which are available, this is possibly one of the best as it will eliminate sarocoptic mange, fleas, lice and similar ectoparasites. It has a GBH gamma benzene hexachloride BP base. ICI Tetmosel, whilst developed for human use as a cure for scabies, is equally as good for dogs and the owner can have the added pleasure of seeing the expressions on fellow customer's faces as he asks for such a preparation at the local chemist's.

An animal which is constantly working, either as a beating dog on the nearby shoot or as a companion on rabbiting forays, could benefit from the use of a liquid antiseptic upon reaching home

ough-coated terriers sometimes sustain wounds and injuries vhich may, because of the density of coat, go unnoticed. Minor uts and wounds will generally improve by regular swabbing with ome form of suitable disinfectant.

each evening. A terrier with a rough or woolly coat could receive wounds which, because of the thickness of the coat, may go unnoticed so the use of an antiseptic such as TCP or Savlon will prevent these injuries from festering.

## Fits and Convulsions

Occasionally, a hard-working terrier may be seen to collapse whilst out in the field. This is obviously very worrying to the owner, who should seek immediate veterinary attention. If the collapse is a result of a fit rather than a serious heart attack, it is likely that the dog will recover very quickly and may appear to be in perfect condition upon reaching home. He could, unfortunately, have another fit at any time as convulsions are often hereditary, associated with inter-breeding. They can recur at intervals of hours, days, weeks or months but, once diagnosed, drugs can very effectively control the situation. When present at the first collapse, although panic will, understandably, prevent any rational thinking on your part, you should try and remember that there is the possibility of the collapse being a result of poisoning and the precautions outlined in the section of Chapter 3 which deals specifically with this problem should be brought into action.

## Administering Drugs

If the vet has, for whatever ailment, prescribed drugs in tablet form there is often a difficulty in administering the cure. There are two methods normally used by dog owners, the first being to pull back the dog's head, open the jaws with one hand and place the tablet at the back of the tongue and then hold the jaws firmly closed. The other hand can then be used to stroke the throat which normally ensures that the dog swallows the pill. The second method is to merely place the medicine in the terrier's food as, since they seldom chew their food, this addition may go unnoticed. Some, however, develop an uncanny knack of eating round the small particle of food in which the tablet is hidden and then there will be no alternative but to resort to the first method.

# BREEDING PUPPIES

## A Health Check Before Mating

A bitch usually comes into season twice yearly and it is generally reckoned that you should not breed from her until the second season at the earliest. This gives you ample opportunity to mark down the expected dates of all the periods when she is due to come into season and work out exactly when it is convenient for you to have a litter of puppies. There is no point, for example, in mating your terrier and then realising that there is a family holiday booked a week after the pups are due to be born.

A few weeks before she is expected to come on heat, make an appointment with your vet and ask him to check her over. If the bitch has any traces of worms or irritations which will require treatment, now is the time to carry them out, not when she is expecting as, to give drugs then, may cause deformities in the unborn puppies. Overweight bitches stand a good chance of being temporarily infertile and the veterinary surgeon will be able to advise on the ideal weight for your dog.

## Selecting the Right Bitch and Stud Dog

No matter how wonderful you happen to feel your terrier bitch is, do not use her for breeding if it is known that she has a serious fault as breeding will only perpetuate it and the fault will almost certainly appear in the resultant offspring. You should always keep at the back of your mind the fact that you are trying to improve on the bitch or, at the very least, maintain the same standard, as there is no other reason for maintaining a particular blood line. Do not fall into the same trap as so many others and think that you are going to make a profit from the eventual sale of the progeny as, by the time they have reached the age of seven or eight weeks, the money which you can ask for a non-pedigree dog is not likely to do more than repay the vet's fees and food costs incurred from the rearing of the puppies.

Furthermore if you, as the owner of a potential stud dog, are approached by the owner of a bitch and, for one reason or another, you feel that it would be an unsuitable mating, you must not be frightened of saying so. A great deal of thought must go into choosing a dog which will be suitable for a particular bitch and every aspect of its physical make-up, working ability and temperament should be considered. No one, it must be admitted, can prophesy with any degree of certainty the outcome of a particular mating but if there is to be any hope of success, the choice of dog is every bit as important as breeding from the right bitch.

There is an unfortunate tendency for the owners of a bitch to go to the top dog of the working terrier show circuit but, unless he is also a proven worker, this is

Even though you may own an ideal stud dog, if you feel that mating it with an inferior bitch would lessen the breed's potential, you should refuse the offer of a stud arrangement.

likely to weaken the sporting attributes of the bitch. This is where the records kept by reputable breeders come in useful and you could do worse than approach the breeder of your own bitch and ask him for advice on line breeding or a suitable outcross. Most would advise that the bitch should not be put to any member of her family closer than an uncle as to do more than this results in line breeding becoming in-breeding and without expert understanding of genetics, which the first-time breeder is unlikely to possess, highly-strung, nervy and fault-laden puppies are likely to be the eventual result.

If the dog's breeding is similar but not too close to that of your own bitch, there is a far greater chance of producing good puppies than if you take the bitch to a completely unrelated stud dog. Even when it is decided to outcross, there should still be, somewhere in the records, a dog who is at the very least half-brother to a dog or bitch on the dam's side. In the opinion of most successful breeders, an outcross mating should be carried out perhaps once in every three generations as this will retain all the good points already achieved but the new blood will give added strength and improvement to the weakening genes.

You should never be tempted into cross breeding – that is, say your dog is one of the Jack Russell type and you like the working ability and temperament but do not like the colour so you are tempted into mating him with a Lakeland because you feel that some of the pups will have an attractive black and tan coat. It is likely that the good points on either side will be dispelled as a result of this mating and there is a possibility that all the pups could turn out to have white coats but have the more aggressive temperament and working characteristics of the Lakeland. This is, it must be admitted, very unlikely but a hypothetical case like this serves as an example.

You may be tempted into cross breeding in order to miniaturise the resultant offspring, but, in extreme cases, the progeny's body may become too heavy for the leg size as, although it is possible to scale down the terrier's overall aspects, it is not possible to scale down knees and other joints with the result that you achieve dwarfism. (In human dwarfs, it is noticeable that, whilst the head and body are of normal size, arms and legs are not.) This type of breeding could cause patella luxation, perhaps better known as 'slipping stifle', which is most prevalent in terriers which are under twelve inches (twenty-five centimetres) at the shoulder. It is most often noticed in ageing dogs by the unmistakeable 'one-two-three, hop' as they walk.

Beagles have, over several centuries, suffered from 'dwarfism'. Unlike many terrier breeds, however, they have not developed 'Queen Anne' legs and impracticable under-developed knee-joints.

## Mating

As already stated, the bitch comes into season approximately once every six months and lasts for twenty-one days with the maximum period of fertility occurring between day nine and day fourteen. Although it is possible for a successful mating to be carried out at any time during this fertile period, day eleven is usually considered to be the optimum. Having said this, the first successful mating of my present terrier bitch was carried out on the sixteenth day as prior to this she simply refused to accept the dog and so it can be seen that there are no hard and fast rules. Be on the lookout for trouble if there are male dogs wandering in your vicinity as it has been known for a successful mating to take place through weld mesh, the bitch being very accommodating and thrusting her rear end close enough to the wire for the dog to have his evil way with her!

The physical signs of when a bitch is coming on heat are a slight swelling of the vulva from which appears a light bloody discharge. This will eventually become clear fluid and, by the eleventh day, if you stroke or scratch the bitch around the base of her tail, it will be noticed that she stands with her tail well over to one side. She is at this stage, very definitely, ready for mating.

The actual mating procedure is not, necessarily, an easy operation, especially if one or both terriers are inexperienced. If the bitch is small and the dog longer on the leg, it may pay to hold the bitch's back end slightly off the ground. This works well with an experienced dog but does, it has to be admitted, put off a younger, inexperienced animal. The owners should not become anxious as this will undoubtedly transfer itself to the dogs. The best way to effect a mating, at least as an initial approach, is to put both dog and bitch in a loose box or garden shed, let them run about and get to know each other but keep your eye on them without interfering. If the bitch stands but then gets frustrated due to the inexpertise of the stud dog, or the dog himself shows very little interest, do not leave them too long before parting them and trying them again the following day.

It is not, as so many people seem to think, necessary for a 'tie' to take place for the mating to be successful, but it is usually the eventual outcome. This tie can last a considerable length of time and the dog will effect this by mounting the bitch in the conventional way before turning himself round to face the opposite direction to the bitch. During this period, the sperm is flowing from the dog to the bitch and obviously indicates the likelihood of a more successful mating than one which is over in a matter of seconds or minutes.

I have seen it written that after mating, the bitch should not be worked or given any strenuous exercise for a few days as there is a faint danger of her returning the sperm – but surely, once the egg has been fertilised, there can be no turning back? There is, however, no doubt that once the bitch has been mated, she needs some special care.

## Caring for the In-Whelp Bitch

The gestation period is nine weeks or, to be more exact, sixty-three days. Normal exercise can be continued up to around five weeks at which time, depending on how many pups the bitch is carrying, she should begin to show signs of being pregnant.

It is not unknown, when the mating has been unsuccessful, or when the bitch has not even been mated, for her to have a swollen abdomen and carry blankets or newspapers around making nests. Even though she may also produce milk in her teats, it may just be the result of a phantom pregnancy, a condition to which some bitches are very prone, especially a few weeks after being in season. The condition may need to be controlled by hormone injections and, in extreme cases, a hysterectomy will eventually become necessary.

Assuming that all is well, a bitch which seems to be in whelp should be fed twice daily from around six weeks into the pregnancy and it is essential to ensure that she is receiving plenty of vitamin D. (Bonemeal, sterilised or not, is of no real use in this situation.) Additives must include both calcium and phosphorus plus a course of multivitamins which will help to redress any natural imbalance in the food. Do not think that the addition of cod-liver oil will remedy all potential problems, indeed too much at this stage will induce symptoms similar to rickets and care should be taken not to make too much use of this normally useful standby.

## Whelping Day

Before whelping day, the bitch should be made acquainted with her whelping box which can be made from plywood or three plain boards laid together to make a platform sufficiently roomy for her to stretch at full length. This should be raised three inches (seven centimetres) from the floor level and provided with a wooden lip on the outer side which should be about six inches (fifteen centimetres) in height. There is, however, no guarantee that the bitch will whelp in this specially designed box and I once had one which refused to give birth anywhere but on the spare bed with my wife holding her paw for comfort! If the whelping is likely to occur in cold weather, the addition of an infra-red pig lamp suspended about one metre from the floor, will help in keeping the puppies warm.

When several dogs are kept, try and kennel the in-whelp bitch well away from them and the resultant distractions, especially if this is her first litter. Whelping in maiden bitches is frequently accompanied by restlessness for as long as forty-eight hours before commencement. Such animals should be given plenty of time to settle – lay out some newspapers in the box so that she can scratch them up together and make a nest. These can be burned after the pups are born and replaced as often as necessary.

In his excellent book *The Terrier's Vocation* Geoffrey Sparrow suggests that the hair should be clipped from the 'bearing and inner buttocks', and this area washed with soap and water. He also advises washing the teats, believing that this will prevent the bitch from spreading roundworm to her puppies. It is now thought that the roundworm larvae lie dormant in the bitch's bloodstream, only becoming active again when she is pregnant, and they then enter the body of the foetus via the bloodstream.

The first pup should arrive about two hours after real labour pains have first been noticed and the intervals between the puppies can be most irregular. If you are on hand (and it is advisable during the first whelping) and there has been an interval of more than four hours since

It is sometimes thought that washing the teats of an in-whelp bitch will help in preventing the spread of Roundworm to the pups.

the last puppy but the bitch is obviously in some stage of discomfort, indicating that there are more pups to come, the vet should be called as there could be a puppy blocking the entrance to the cervix. A greeny-coloured discharge which suddenly appears may indicate that there is a dead pup inside and once again, the vet should be called immediately.

The bitch should, by instinct alone, chew through the umbilical cord and, provided that she is not too upset by your presence, you should move the puppy closer to her head so that she can lick them off and stimulate them into life. She will probably attempt to eat the placenta and should not be discouraged from doing this as it is thought that it contains certain nutrients which aid the milk flow.

When asking terrier breeders for their opinions concerning the birth, some have told me that it is better not to bother with any offspring which the bitch discards as it is likely to be a runt which will eventually die or have to be culled when it is pushed away from the milk source by its stronger and fitter siblings. From personal experience, however, this is not always the case and I remember one first born which a bitch ignored. It appeared to be dead when we found it, but was revived by being placed in a box in the warming cupboard of the Rayburn, and went on to be everyone's 'pick of the litter'.

The bitch should, from now on, be fed on high protein feeds if she is to provide sufficient milk for the puppies to do well.

## CARING FOR THE PUPPIES

The bitch will care for the puppies for the first week or so and will do an admirable job without any intervention or interference from the owner. On the fourth day, the puppies' tails and dew claws should receive attention.

### Tail Docking

On BBC Radio Four's *Punters* programme (17 March 1988) the 'barbaric' question of tail docking was raised. In order to add spice to the interview, there was a 'sound over' of puppies squealing as their tails were docked. In the following programme a week later, it seemed that literally hundreds of listeners had rung the BBC saying how distressed their own pets had been when hearing the sound of the pups. Distress was apparently evident in those dogs who had themselves had their tails docked when young. A veterinary surgeon to whom the programme's host spoke, offered the explanation that any dog has a good memory recall and that the sound of the puppies complaining while having their tails cut had re-awakened the pain which the listener's dogs had felt when their own tails were docked.

I offer no comment to this, save that of saying that a working dog which is bred to enter thick cover, and I am thinking of spaniels as well as terriers, will probably suffer more discomfort through the damage caused in rough conditions than it will in the few moments it is necessary to take in docking a young puppy. The 'old school' used to bite off the puppies' tails with their teeth but I am pleased to say that things have progressed a little since then!

Unless you know a competent breeder who will come and do the job for you, the tail and dew claws should be removed by a vet. The British Veterinary Association and the Royal College of Veterinary Surgeons are, however, opposed to the docking of all puppies. All that is in fact required is a quick cut and perhaps a stitch or two. I have seen laymen use a razor blade or even a pair of sharp secateurs, the cut being followed by a dab of disinfectant. A stitch is not really necessary. Most people take off dew claws at the same time as they dock, feeling that these claws (which are found immediately above the foot) serve no useful purpose and can, indeed, cause problems in later life. If, however, they are left but kept short by means of an occasional trimming, they may never cause trouble at any stage of the terrier's life.

In gamekeeping, it is necessary to stop growing pheasants from pecking each other. At the age of three weeks you can either fit plastic bits between the upper and lower mandibles which prevent the wearer from taking hold of his neighbour's feathers or remove the pointed part of the upper beak by means of a special tool which holds a sharp blade and is heated by means of a car battery. This cuts and cauterises at the same time and I have often wondered whether it would not be possible to develop a similar piece of apparatus for docking puppies' tails. This would, at the very least, mean that the operation was bloodless.

Whatever method is used, it pays to remove half the number of puppies from the nest, leaving the remainder with the bitch. Take them well away before docking just on the off chance that one may squeal and upset the bitch. Once the deed has been done, return this half of the pups and take out the rest taking care not to let any of the puppies be in a situation where they may get chilled. Docking is, of course, unnecessary in the Scottish, Border or Bedlington terriers. This fact does, I suppose, throw some real doubt on the need to dock at all, as any of these three breeds should, provided that they are of a working strain, be capable of pushing through cover every bit as well as a docked breed.

## Growing Puppies

At the fourth week, the puppies' teeth begin to pierce the gums and weaning is generally commenced in the fifth week. At this time it is normal for the bitch to vomit pre-digested food which the pups should be allowed to eat as this is nature's way of ensuring that the food is already partially digested.

At first, any food which is given to them by the owner should be in the form of a substitute for the mother's milk and

Docking is unnecessary in the Scottish Terrier.

evaporated milk can be used with great success at this stage. It must not, however, be fed to puppies once they reach the age of four months as the rennin which effectively coagulates milk in the puppies' stomach disappears at this stage of the animal's growth.

A proprietary brand of lactol which, like any other milk substitute, should be warmed to blood temperature is also useful and is administered at first by means of dipping your fingers into the solution and encouraging the puppies to lick from them. After a couple of days, they will be capable of lapping from a dish, which should be one which is not easily upturned. At the beginning of the sixth week, you can begin to introduce a little green tripe (provided that it is minced), cooked meat, cereal and milk or even one of the soft, flaky, all-in-one type of adult foods. The puppies should, at this stage, be taking four small meals a

day which can be reduced to three at the age of three months. At four months, two meals should be enough until, at around a year old, it should be possible to reduce feeding to a once daily event. If you reduce the number of daily meals too quickly, serious digestive problems will undoubtedly occur.

Puppies are born with intestinal parasites which are carried through their mother's bloodstream. Until the age of around four weeks, the pup carries some immunity from any serious problems which it gains from the dam. By the age of four weeks, any worms which they may have been harbouring will begin to consume vital nutrients from the daily food intake and so another visit to the vet will be necessary in order to purchase a suitable puppy wormer.

It is not unusual to see young pups with a hernia protruding from its abdomen but, provided that it is caught early

117

enough, it should be possible to push back the offending part of the intestine by means of this simple remedy. At the age of about four weeks, place a small coin (a one-penny piece) over the protrusion and, very gently and carefully, push it inwards towards the stomach before taping it tightly with sticking plaster. After a few days, the tissues should have grown over and be holding the offending part in its correct position. If it is noticed that the bitch attempts to remove the plaster, a few drops of strong smelling perfume dropped on to the tape should prevent any future efforts on her part. Do not, however, inadvertently let any drops fall on the puppies' skin tissues as it may cause some irritation or even burning.

## From Six Weeks Onwards

There has, in the past, been a tendency for breeders to sell on their puppies at the age of six weeks but this is too early,

a fact which most people now realise. In any case, if you intend to keep a dog as an addition to the home kennel, there is no rush as you cannot hope to make a serious 'pick of the litter' until at least six to seven months of age. It would be very disheartening to make your choice at seven or eight weeks and then, twelve months later, see one of the pups which you discarded sweeping the board at a local show or working better than the one which you decided to keep.

By the end of the sixth week the bitch should be removed from the litter for the whole of the day. The length of time which she has been spending away from the pups will, of course, have been increasing gradually from perhaps four weeks of age and the bitch herself will probably decide when, and for how long, her puppies can be left. You should not be tempted into allowing the bitch back to her puppies after the end of the sixth week as, by this time, her milk will have begun to dry up and re-

Seven-week-old Jack Russell puppies.

118

introducing her and letting the pups suckle will encourage her once again to lactate.

Some litters of pups turn out to be very aggressive even at this early stage of their development and need to be separated for their own safety. As with adult terriers, they should not be kennelled in any more than twos, for if three are kept together the stronger two will gang up on the third, weaker animal with the result that it will be maimed or even killed. For the same reason, it is suggested that the offspring of different litters should never be mixed in order to save space or make life easier for the owner. Puppies as young as ten weeks of age already seem to have inherited the killing instinct but will go for the bowel area rather than the throat and it has been known for them to rip out the stomach of their unfortunate victim.

## Selecting Which Puppy to Keep

Many of the pointers I suggested that you should follow when choosing your first ever puppy in Chapter 1, obviously apply when deciding which dog to keep from your first litter. By this stage, however, you will be more experienced and therefore in a better position to make a sounder judgement.

You should, of course, be looking for a puppy which will attain a higher standard than the brood bitch as there can be no point in progressing with a bloodline which is not aiming towards perfection. Unless you intend to go into terrier breeding in a big way, it is unlikely that you will retain a dog in preference to a bitch as you could not use the son on the bitch already in your possession. So, unless it proves to be an outstanding worker, it will be a useless addition.

Generally, the rough-coated Jack Russell is favoured and most judges pick a rough-coated terrier as their 'Best in Show'. Already, then, we have two criteria and we have not even considered the finer points of an individual puppy. If a terrier is the right height, has the right depth of chest with plenty of lung room and stands well forward on its toes, it matters very little as to its colour but, as a general rule, you should try and stick to the marking standards laid down by the particular breed society. This is perhaps more important when speaking of the Jack Russell type as interested parties are now beginning to show great concern in creating a type which is comparable to the Parson's original dog, rather than accept any short-legged, thick-boned, bow-fronted creature. There is now no reason why you should not attempt to breed an animal which is white and broken-coated but has two brown eye patches (badger-faced) and a mark about the size of a two penny piece at the base of the tail.

If it is a first litter, please approach a reputable breeder for his advice on which puppy to keep as, although the best of a newcomer's litter is not likely to come up to the standards which he or she requires, nevertheless they will undoubtedly remember their first brood of pups and be able to give some constructive criticism. If the expert offers to buy a particular puppy, hang on to it as he has obviously seen some great potential in the dog! I know one experienced breeder who was asked to look through a litter bred by another person with a great knowledge of terriers who, because too big an interest was shown in a certain dog, refused to sell it. It was only when the breeder of the litter died, that it was possible to buy the dog from

The Jack Russell public house is situated opposite the entrance to the church in which Parson John Russell preached. The popularity of the breed probably explains the change of name from the 'New Inn'.

his widow. This went on to win many shows and sire countless numbers of very presentable progeny.

## Finding Homes for the Rest

There are bound to be some individuals in any litter which need to be passed on. Having picked the best, there may still be one or two good representatives of the particular breed left and these should be sold without too much difficulty to interested terrier people who have heard of the presence of a litter via the local grapevine. Other pups which will never make either a good show or working dog may be sold cheaply to someone who merely wishes to own a terrier as a pet. However, the breeder has a responsibility to ensure that they will be well looked after and not used by unscrupulous people who will try and mate them in order to make a profit whilst, at the same time, lowering the breeding standards which they should be attempting to achieve.

In every litter, there is almost bound to be a runt and this should be eradicated as soon as its faults become apparent. There is no point in artificially rearing such a dog in the hope that it will miraculously improve and it is far better to become hardened to the fact that there will be occasions when a pup has to be 'put down' both for its own good and that of the breed.

## Names and Naming

The choice of name is generally a matter of personal preference but it is nevertheless interesting to note that when names of winners at a terrier show are read out, the majority of the list contains short and easily-called names. These have been in common usage amongst terrier owners for many years: Nick, Nip, Rock, Rebel, Judy, Nettle, Grip and Tod

Tess, a Lakeland terrier, named as so many others have been through countless generations.

(the Cumbrian word for fox) are still as popular as they were fifty years ago. Some breeders follow the fashion set by the hunting fraternity and give the pups of each litter a name beginning with the same initial as the dams. Thus, if the bitch is known as Dauntless her pups could be called, Diver, Duchess, Dipper, Diligence or Daffodil. The idea behind this is to allow hunt staff to recognise immediately the breeding of an individual hound and, if a different initial is used yearly, they can also recall in just which year an animal was born.

If you intend to go into terrier breeding in a big way, this method of identification may prove useful. If not, simply pick a name which appeals.

# 8 Psychology, Law and a Final Word

## PSYCHOLOGY

As with any breed of dog it is vital that the terrier owner tries to understand exactly what is going on in the animal's mind. It is all too easy to anthropomorphise and, because of their apparent ability to understand, credit terriers with being responsible for all their actions. In actual fact, nothing could be further from the truth even though the aim of training is to control bodily actions through the medium of the dog's mind.

One of the first requirements is to become the centre of interest to the dog and this is why so many professional gundog trainers insist on their animals being kennelled when not out training or exercising. A lack of attention may arise from many circumstances, some of which can be attributed to fear of the owner, being too immature, boredom or even ill-health.

### Instinct

The inherited tendency to kill is obviously required in a terrier but in its unconditioned state would mean that no family pet or neighbour's cat would be safe, and so it must be modified by experience. An easy illustration would be to point out that the terrier must not kill the children's pet rabbit out on the lawn but is expected to kill a wild rabbit if one escapes from the net whilst ferreting. This lesson can only be learned by spending time with the dog and showing it the tame rabbit, making it very obvious that you are displeased should it show too great an interest. If a young terrier is shown a dead fox and allowed to worry it, instinct says that it can rush in and do the same to a live one down a hole. It will, in the latter situation, obviously get hurt and will not make the same mistake again.

In both cases therefore, instinct has been modified by experience rather than by reasoning. Because of the lack of reasoning power, you cannot be sure that the dog will be safe to leave with a friend's pet rabbit in a different environment or with a fox found in any place other than down a hole. The development of instinct (and intelligence) can be retarded by abuse or misuse. As pointed out elsewhere, a terrier which is beaten upon its return home after running off will, because of this lack of reasoning power, associate the punishment with returning home and so obviously be less eager to come back the next time. It will not, however, be any less eager to run away again because neither instinct nor indeed intelligence will inform it that it was this action which caused the displeasure.

Intelligence works in exactly the way that common sense would lead us to expect and if the terrier's homecoming is greeted with pleasure and satisfaction on the part of the owner, the dog is less likely to wander off or if it does, it will return more readily to hand. To be totally successful, the owner must catch the dog actually in the act of running away and then – but only then – discourage further disappearances by effecting some form of unpleasantness or discomfort. At all times, remember that it is easier to obtain the desired response immediately rather than to allow faults to develop and then try and eradicate them before trying to form new ones.

Where possible, the young terrier should be allowed to try and solve his own problems as this is the quickest way of learning and allowing the dog to develop his instinct and intelligence. Dogs cannot be trained by means of a crash course and if you have any hopes at all of achieving a useful, working ally, an inexhaustible amount of patience is essential. Failures and disappointments should be avoided but are impossible without the owner having at least some understanding of how the terrier's mind works.

## STAYING WITHIN THE LAW

Showing the outside world that you, as a working terrier owner, are prepared to try and understand what goes on inside your animal's head, rather than just treat it as a 'killing tool' will go a long way towards proving that you have some degree of responsibility. In this day and age, there appears to be no shortage of outsiders ready and willing to criticise anyone who shows an interest in using dogs to kill wildlife. The hunting fraternity have long become used to their sport

being disrupted by those who wish to see it abolished and the beagling world in particular have suffered more than most due to their inability to hunt away from any protestors. Foxhunters are undoubtedly more fortunate in the fact that their horses allow them to escape from such attention.

Using terriers for fun is seen by those intent on stopping any form of field sports as an act of barbarism and, although as an individual there is not much hope of being able to fight against organisations which are dedicated to their abolition, it will definitely pay to keep on the right side of the law and not give them any reasons with which to strengthen their argument.

It is perhaps cynical to suggest that you are guilty until proven innocent but the law is very complicated and two acts which appear at first to be identical may, because of a very minor technical point, be worlds apart, one being legal the other not. Without an experienced defence, this point may be impossible to prove or disprove and so the best way of ensuring that you will never be in this unfortunate position, is never to put yourself in a doubtful situation.

The main legal problem likely to occur is if you are working a terrier in the vicinity of a known badger earth, as the badger is protected by both the Badger's Act, 1973 and the amended Wildlife and Countryside Act, 1985. The subject is very technical as it is, for example, not against the law to dig in or around a badger's sett if you can prove that you are only interested in foxes or even rabbits which are also living there. It is, however, an offence to dig in or around a badger's sett if you are digging intentionally for badgers and are not in possession of a relocation licence issued either by the Nature Conservancy Council or the Ministry of Agriculture, Fisheries and Food. These licenses permit the taking of animals where they are proven to be causing serious damage to land, poultry or other property but otherwise no excuse is acceptable.

Employees of the Ministry of Agriculture Fisheries and Food are exempt from obtaining these licences and, because it has been proved that badgers carry bovine tuberculosis, can kill or take the animals in order to prevent the disease from spreading. Initially, they used Cymag but more recently, have taken to giving live vaccines in baits in an effort to see whether this will combat the disease.

It is, however, no defence for the terrier man found with a badger carcass to claim that he had picked it up out of the hedgerow and assumed that its death was a result of MAFF activity, as it is only their operatives who are allowed to remove any bodies – and even they must first obtain authority from the Ministry of Agriculture. It is an offence to be in possession of a whole or part badger unless it can be proved that it had been killed in a road accident or by similar, uncontrollable circumstances.

Digging for foxes is a frequently-used excuse when a terrier man is taken to court after being found in the vicinity of a sett but, whether or not he is telling the truth, this defence will not stand up if he has failed to obtain permission from the landowner or his tenant. This should preferably have been received in writing as is common practice in the foxhunting world – the Master must have permission for his hounds to cross over private land and for his terrier man to dig where deemed necessary. In these circumstances it is likely that the owner/

occupier wishes to rid his ground o foxes but even so, the amateur terrie man cannot assume that he too will have permission to go over the ground the following day. In any case, someone who is prepared to enter land withou permission in order to try his dogs or ground where foxes are known to be found deserves to be caught and prosecuted for trespass at the very least.

I make no apology for frequently returning to the morality of digging out foxes purely for sport as it is important you take responsibility for your actions if the hunting of animals with dogs is to continue. I also recommend that you follow closely the advice given in *Fair Game* by C. Parkes and J. Thornley (Pelham, 1987). This contains information appertaining to the laws of country sports and the protection of wildlife.

There is one final piece of advice to be given before leaving the topic of the law. It is well known that the RSPCA is against any form of hunting and so, in the unfortunate event that you, as a bona fide terrier owner working your dogs with the landowner's permission, get into difficulty and your animals become lost or injured, you should make sure that private veterinary help is sought on site. If this is done and the RSPCA is subsequently called to the scene by an outsider who believes that an act of cruelty is being carried out, they will not interfere when they know that the owner is not committing an offence. Without a veterinary surgeon being called, the RSPCA may try to instigate proceedings which the worried terrier handler could well do without.

John Broadhurst, terrier man to the Crawley and Horsham, with a terrier showing the scars of battle.

## A FINAL WORD: DEDICATION

If you can't do it properly, don't do it at all is a very apt cliché to remember. Dedication, both to the breed and, more importantly, to the individual animal you have chosen, is absolutely vital if you are to achieve the maximum satisfaction from terrier ownership.

## Finance

Fortunately, dedication is not synonymous with expense, and it should be possible, if you are of a naturally thrifty mind, to construct a run and kennel of second-hand but nevertheless sound material costing little or nothing. Food

too, should be fairly inexpensive, especially if you use a terrier to help out with beating on the local shoot and are paid the going beater's rate. By keeping this money to one side, it should be possible to accrue enough finances to keep a single terrier in food and incidentals for the rest of the year. It will not of course, pay for any vet's bills which may be incurred and for this reason it is a sensible idea to take out some form of insurance against the terrier needing veterinary attention. Details of the various plans available can usually be found at your local surgery and, although they cannot be used for expected expenditure such as booster injections or worming tablets, will, nevertheless, prove to be invaluable in the event of serious injury

A cheaply-constructed kennel and run.

or illnesses which require an operation. It is also possible to cover for the loss of a terrier's life on some of these policies but it is often difficult for the owner to assess the true value of his animal.

A non-pedigree terrier pup can be bought relatively cheaply at the age of seven to eight weeks, but it is extremely difficult to put a price on a young dog of around six months of age and virtually impossible to cost a trained and entered adult animal. Much depends on the person from whom you make the purchase. An experienced breeder who has the well-being of a particular breed at heart may be prepared to almost give a terrier away if he knows that it is going to a responsible working home.

I know of one dog which won several important working terrier shows during the summer of 1987 and was seen by a visiting American who first of all offered the dog's owner £500 and then, when he did not accept the offer, increased it to £750. It says a great deal for the credibility of the owner who, despite this lucrative offer, refused to sell as the dog is vital to his future breeding plans.

## Terriers in America

Nowhere is the dedication to the working terrier more obvious than in America where the whole business of showing and working ability is taken very seriously. Not only does a terrier have to look good and show well but it also has to prove its 'gameness' through specially designed working tests. This testing is

American working tests include the use of artificially constructed tunnels made from piping and corrugated iron, at the end of which is placed a cage of tame white rats.

done by means of an artificially constructed underground tunnel, at the end of which is placed a cage containing two or three tame white rats. The terriers are then taken to the testing area by the handler and are expected to mark at the hole before entering. Once up to their quarry, they score further points by barking, thus indicating that they have found it.

Unfortunately, tests of this nature would not be allowed over here, which is perhaps a shame, as it would at least enable show judges to sort out those which work from those which merely look pretty. Judges in America are not allowed to be seen talking to competitors immediately preceding the show in case they are thought to be favouring a particular owner.

Although some breeds of terriers have been exported to the United States of America for several years – the Norfolk, for instance was sent over there in the early 1920s where it became known as the Jones terrier – it is only in recent times that exporting terriers to America has become a commonplace event. It may sound condescending but it seems that no one can breed working dogs like the British and there is a constant demand for gundogs, terriers and especially the English Foxhound. This – and even the Americans themselves admit it – stands out from their own breed as a bantamweight fighter would from a Sumo wrestler. By careful and knowledgeable breeding, they are gradually including exported bloodlines into their own working dogs and, when in doubt,

127

these dedicated breeders are not afraid to come to Britain to ask advice.

## Learning from the 'Experts'

Asking advice is one thing which the newcomer to terrier ownership should not be afraid to do. Despite the many books on the subject, you can only really learn from experience and so it pays to make a friend of a local and respected owner. It is, admittedly, possible to learn from your own mistakes but why not avoid making them by picking the brains of experienced handlers? Provided that you are willing to learn, I have found that most breeders are only too keen to talk to a fellow enthusiast and will readily pass on any information they have gained over the years. Little snippets of information, even if of no practical use, can prove to be fascinating.

Recently, for example, I spoke to a terrier owner who is also kennelman to a nearby pack of hounds. During the course of our conversation on feeding raw meat to terriers he happened to mention that he fed a lot of paunches to the hounds and in the winter, even though they were hunting twice weekly, they put on more weight than in the summer when hounds normally expect to live a rather indolent life. The reason behind this weight increase was, in the kennelman's opinion, due to the fact that the livestock casualties from which the paunches were taken were fed on concentrates in the winter and therefore the paunches contained more in the way of nutrients and protein than in the summer when the animals were kept entirely on grass.

It is also possible to pick up little labour-saving tips on your visits to other people's kennels, and ideas which they

You should never be afraid of asking the experts' opinion. The late Ted Adsett with some of his terriers.

have found to work can often be adapted for use in your home situation. Obviously if you are only keeping a couple of terriers, there is no need to operate in the same way as large breeders with a couple of dozen animals in their establishment. Never allow yourself to be carried away by their enthusiasm and end up keeping so many terriers that it becomes impossible to look after them properly.

## How Many Terriers?

In the majority of cases, such as in beating, ratting, rabbiting or merely mouching, one terrier is generally sufficient for the needs of the average owner and with this one-to-one relationship, a

How many terriers you should own depends on how much work you expect to carry out.

bond between the two will quickly appear. For the first-time terrier handler there is much to be learned from the dog and it is often said by trainers who are experienced in various working breeds that it is necessary to ruin a dog before getting a good one. It is perhaps an unkind remark but nevertheless, there is some truth in it and a person who is genuinely interested in any sporting dog will train his second animal from mistakes made with his first.

Even if you do not intend to breed from your terrier, there will, however, come a time when it is necessary to think about replacing the single dog. All too often this decision is left far too late and you should not delay it until the original terrier is retired from work before purchasing a replacement.

Despite the fact that terriers are notoriously aggressive towards each other and that this aggression is bound to be accentuated in a situation whereby the original terrier has been 'cock o' the midden' for many years, the introduction of a young puppy is possible provided that adequate care is taken to avoid jealousy. This is more easily achieved in a kennel environment than when the dog in question is part of a household as, if space allows, they can be kennelled separately. This is not always so easy in a house where, if two dogs take an instant dislike to each other, it may be necessary to keep doors permanently closed.

When first bringing a puppy home, do not allow members of the family to make so much of a fuss that the older terrier feels neglected and excluded, as this is sure to create jealousy. Introduce one to the other but try not to let the youngster get over exuberant. Take the puppy out separately but not at the times when you have normally taken out the older dog;

129

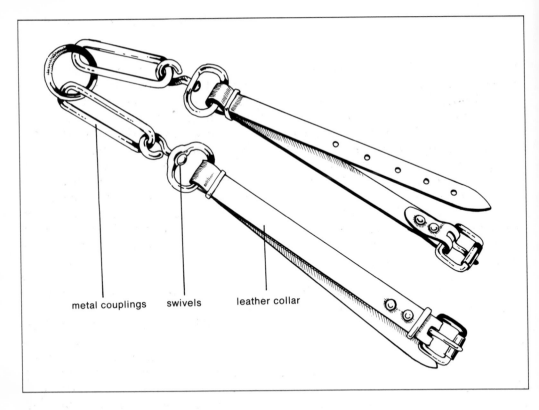

metal couplings    swivels    leather collar

A pair of terrier couplings. The collars are connected to a single
lead by a metal device which gives the wearers freedom by means
of swivel mechanisms. These are particularly useful when
accustoming a young terrier to his older 'teacher'.

maintain this routine and settle the pup
into a new regime until it is possible to
take both out together. These solitary
periods can be used to get to know the
puppy better and to begin a little early
training. Provided that the training in
question is not too competitive, when,
for instance, the young dog is showing a
certain reluctance to enter thick cover,
the older animal can prove a useful ally
in showing the young terrier just what is
required.

The number of terriers which will
eventually be required should you
become terrier man to the local hunt
depends on a great many things, not the
least of which is the amount of days

hounds spend hunting. In the rough,
three-day-a-week country, where digging is a frequent occurrence, two cou-
ples would not be too many as injuries
and ill-health may mean that two terriers
are incapacitated at any one time. It
used to be the fashion for hunt kennels
to contain 'oversized' terriers which
were used against badgers but hunts
today seem well able to cope with one
type of terrier and there is no need for
anyone to have different dogs for different jobs.

Geoffrey Sparrow, writing in a pri-
vately published edition of *The Terrier's
Vocation* (1949), thought that is was
advisable to:

'. . .collect or breed a few good terriers. . . using a small dog with a good nose to find another perhaps not so good, to carry on for a while and – in badger digging – a strong hard dog to "bag-up" with, for when the badger is facing one, it is a great comfort to have a "Caesar" dog handy. If a dog is very small he may make a good "pipe-cleaner" and such are very valuable and scarce, for foxes, and particularly cubs, can enter an earth or drain that an ordinary dog cannot negotiate, and indeed may be considered capable of entering any place where they can put their head.'

## Making a Note

The truly dedicated terrier enthusiast should keep a diary or notebook to remind himself of various happenings throughout the year. As a diary, such a book proves a useful means of remembering when a visit to the vet is due or, if involved with beating or hunting, the forthcoming fixture dates; but, as a record to which to refer in future years, it is invaluable. When using your terrier on the shoot it will be interesting to see how many days were spent beating in any particular season, what the weather conditions were like and what the total bag was at the end of the day. Interesting nature notes can also be included as, whilst beating, you are bound to see flora and fauna which may otherwise pass unnoticed on a normal country walk.

By making a note of the eventual winners at a local show (which can be transferred from the pencil marks made on the schedule), you will begin to recognise some useful-looking terriers which it may be possible to use as stud dogs should you decide to breed from your

A potential show winner.

own bitch. If, as a result of conversation, it turns out that this particular dog is a distant relative of your bitch, this is indeed a bonus and the chances of eventually producing a perfect terrier are greatly enhanced.

Ferreting and rabbiting exploits can be recorded. Not only will the number of rabbits accounted for prove to be of interest but so too will notes made as to the difficulty of digging in certain places. A rough plan of the approximate location of hidden holes will help in preventing escapes on future visits. With a little thought, a diary can be bought large enough to hold photographs of your terriers, maybe some show schedules and a list of friends with whom you have shared some enjoyable outings. On a yearly basis, it will soon build up into a comprehensive library which can be referred to and experiences re-lived in later years. Who knows, it may be discovered a hundred years hence and used to explain the development of the working terrier to forthcoming generations!

## Snippets from the Past

The information gained from those who had the foresight to write down their experiences with working terriers over the years proves both fascinating and amusing. There is, for instance, part of a Norfolk folksong, *A Setter for the Squire* which in the first verse, states:

'A terrier for the labourer
and other simple folk,
For ratting in the stackyard
And rabbits down the yoke.'

John H. Vine, contributing a piece on otter hunting to *The House on Sport*

(1899), described the activities when an otter had gone to ground:

'The hounds are now at a holt in the bank, probably under some old pollard willow: put the terrier in, he must be at home, the hounds are so frantic. Yes, what a hubbub in the bowels of the earth. The poor little dog is getting it hot, I am afraid, and is as likely as not to come out eventually with half an ear gone.'

Charles St John, in *Wild Sports of the Highlands* (1863), indicated a further use for terriers not described in this book,:

'In tracking wounded deer I have occasionally seen a Skye Terrier of very great use, leading his master quietly and with very great precision, up to the place concealing himself; appearing too to be acting more for the benefit of his master, and to show the game, than for his own amusement. I have no doubt that a clever Skye terrier would in many cases get the sportsman a second shot at a wounded deer with more certainty than almost any other kind of dog'

Yet, in Siegfried Sassoon's classic, *Memoirs of a Foxhunting Man* (1928), apart from mentioning that he, (Sassoon) was 'Welcomed by barks from an elderly Aberdeen and slim white fox terrier', and that 'they told me at the 'Bull' last night that he's a great one for terriers and digging out foxes', there is very little discussion on terrier work. Bearing in mind the fact that, in the heyday of hunting, terriers were an essential part of the scene, this is surprising.

Some early writings were amusing as

well as informative, witness a list of necessary equipment required by Jacques du Fouilloux in *La Venerie* (1560):

'Seigneurs who wish to hunt with terriers must be equipped with all things necessary. First a half-dozen strong men to dig, a half-dozen terriers at least. . . He should have an hair mattress. . . All the posts of the cart should be hung with flagons and bottles and at the back there should be a wooden box full of game fowls, hams and beef tongues. But to return, the seigneur must have. . . a young maid of sixteen or seventeen years to stroke his head with her hands.'

Some writings can be educational but, it must be said, not necessarily practical as can be seen from this little gem by Captain Jocelyn Lucas (*Hunt and Working Terriers*, 1939):

'Some terriers fight like demons. If two terriers have a set-to and there happens to be a stable door, a wall, a fence or a gate handy, take them and hang them over it, one each side. They will soon let go.'

But, perhaps the best piece of writing with which to conclude a book on working terriers is, *The Terrier's Song* by D. P. Todd of Kendal and it is frequently sung, to the tune *Laal Melbreak*, whenever a group of fell hunters get together:

*Now there's many a song about hunting,*
*Packs and huntsmen are honoured by name.*
*But there isn't a song about terriers*
*Which in Lakeland have gained lasting fame.*

Chorus:

*So always remember your terriers,*
*Protect them from wet and from cold,*
*For the love of a tyke for his master*
*Can never be measured in gold.*

*Whether its Fury or Trixie or Nellie,*
*Or Rock, Jock or Turk it's the same,*
*One quality you'll find among them,*
*And dalesfolk call it "dead game".*
*And whether he's rough or smooth-coated*
*He'll tackle badger, otter or fox,*
*Run a drain or creep into a soil-hole,*
*Or squeeze through a grike in the rocks.*
Chorus

*He'll yield not one inch though they maul him,*
*He'll fight to the death on his own,*
*Though sometimes he'll be imprisoned*
*By a rush-in of soil or of stone.*
*And then the brave lads of the valleys*
*To save him will toil day or night,*
*And join in the Hallo of triumph*
*As he blinks back to God's blessed light.*
Chorus

*Now at Cruft's famous show down in London,*
*They have Lakelands that aren't worth the name.*
*If you showed 'em a fox or an otter*
*They'd fly for their lives without shame.*
*They're not built to creep or do battle,*
*But to sit on a chair in a house,*
*And they do say that one recent champion*
*Was chased down the road by a mouse!*
Chorus

So here's to our gallant laal workers
Not beauties, perhaps, but they'll do.
With gameness they've also affection.
And make you a pal good and true.
And when your terrier, in old age, is
dying,
And the world all about you seems
sad.
A lick on the hand will console you,
For a truer friend man never had.'

# Appendix 1

## TERRIER CLUBS

Sooner or later, the new terrier enthusiast will want to join some form of club in order to meet fellow terrier owners, participate in any local shows, or, as most clubs are very strong on the social side, merely to have a bit of fun! If you choose a breed which is recognised by the Kennel Club, then all of these particular breeds are likely to have their own club or society, but I personally feel that you will get much more from joining one which deals with the working terrier in general rather than one which is mainly concerned with the dog as a breed.

The Fox Terrier Club, founded in 1876, was probably the first ever club to be entirely devoted to the well-being of a working breed and, during the ensuing fifty years or so, was joined by many others. Most of these societies were formed with the sole purpose of trying the members' terriers against badgers. The Parson Jack Russell Club (not the one which is in existence today) was originally a badger-digging club where, for the annual subscription of a guinea and a daily 'cap' of two shillings and sixpence which was used to pay for the services of diggers, any breed of terrier would be allowed to participate in an organised dig. Today's clubs are, thankfully, less barbaric and would not dream of organising a 'dig' merely to provide a spectator sport or as a means of testing terriers.

There are, however, many reasons why you may need to dig on an individual basis – helping out a local farmer or gamekeeper for instance – and membership of any club in general, but the Fell and Moorland Working Terrier club in particular, will always prove useful should any form of trouble arise. Those owners who might otherwise experience difficulty in finding places to try out their terriers will undoubtedly find their opportunities enhanced upon membership as it is more likely that a farmer or landowner who is having problems with a fox or litter of cubs will approach his local working terrier society for assistance than he would a total stranger about whom he knows nothing. Any society has, therefore, a great deal to lose if it does not insist that its members adhere very rigidly to certain rules and should, at the very least, insist that its members have permission to work over privately-owned land.

By becoming a member of a club, the novice will undoubtedly learn a great deal from his fellows and in a much quicker time than he would if he plodded along in his own sweet way. There can be no substitute for experience and, whether it be in the matter of showing and breeding poultry, hunting, terrier or gundog work, I have found that without exception those who are experienced are only too pleased to pass on their hard-earned information to others. If you wish to begin breeding your own particular strain of working terrier, then the right blood lines, suitable outcrosses and follow-up matings are all available within the membership of the club. You will also find ample opportunity to show your dogs and again useful contacts are bound to be made whilst engaged in this activity.

Finally, the social side of any club cannot be ignored. Do attend the inevitable fund raising events as, by doing so, you will not only enjoy yourself (hopefully!) but also help to ensure the continuation of the club. This will in turn keep your personal subscription to a minimum and, in those societies which offer fringe benefits such as legal assistance if you inadvertently fall foul of the law or have the misfortune to get a terrier stuck fast whilst out working, provide the financial wherewithal.

## The Fell and Moorland Working Terrier Club

For a small annual membership fee there are many benefits to be gained from becoming a member of this society. First and foremost is the ability to show your terrier in one of their area events. As a result of well attended local shows, the organisers are able to forward all of the money thus generated to the Club's central fund and, together with annual subscriptions, this seems to create sufficient finance to be able to offer adequate help should any individual require assistance in the field.

Showing is all very well but it should be remembered that the Fell and Moorland Terrier Club originated in 1966 as a rescue service and it is this fact which puts this particular organisation above all others. Although it is known by the title of 'Fell and Moorland', this was simply because terrier owners in the fell areas were more likely to require assis-

tance as the ground over which they were working was more impenetrable when it was felt necessary to dig. Owners in the West, East or South of the country are nowadays just as likely to receive excellent attention.

In the unfortunate event of your terrier becoming stuck, membership of the club acts as a form of insurance, and the owner of an animal which has become fast can get in touch with a local representative who will, provided that the owner has obtained prior permission from the person who owns the ground, organise the necessary machinery. When help is needed, the area rep contacts the nearest contractor. They do not need to have admitted to an interest in working terriers as they will be paid on the usual hourly basis but it has been found that even those drivers with half an eye on the potential overtime soon become more interested in the welfare of the trapped animal than in any financial remuneration.

From the central fund, a small sum per member is allowed to each area and this covers the cost of any likely call-outs, as 90 per cent of terrier owners belonging to the club never get their animal stuck. Members in the Pennine areas are more likely to require assistance due to the rock formations found in that particular locality, whereas those who work in sandy or easily-dug parts of the country find themselves in the fortunate position of never having to approach the club for help in retrieving their terrier. To clarify the situation even further, the Midlands area of the society put £1,000 per annum into the central fund and only spend an average of £200 on rescue, but some other area might, for instance, put in £500 and yet spend £1,000 on rescue work!(Owners are also covered by insurance in case of accidents to their person whilst in the process of rescuing terriers which have become fast. In the event of an accident, the society's insurance company will readily pay out the sum of £10,000.)

The club is, quite rightly, very keen to promote only legitimate terrier work and any members found to be flouting either the club's rules or the laws of the land, will be immediately expelled. Perhaps the most obvious example to give would be that of badger-digging. Contrary to the popular opinion, badgers are not an endangered species. Nevertheless, it is illegal, because of the Wildlife and Countryside Act, 1981, to dig for, or otherwise disturb, a badger.

Should a member become unfairly accused of some misdemeanour, the club can organise private insurance which would, in the event of a court case, pay legal costs of up to £25,000. (An important fact relating to this is that, should the case go against the member, the club will not pay any fines thus incurred.) Like any rescue work which may be necessary, help in finding a solicitor can be obtained via the local area representative who is likely to prove more useful than the Club's overall secretary.

Finally, the Fell and Moorland Working Terrier Club are very keen to be seen as a respectable group. Although every aspect of the organisation is carried out as a voluntary scheme they are careful to run the society on a very correct basis. There is an executive committee with a sub-committee answerable to the overall body. The area organisations also submit a full set of accounts annually, but perhaps the most important factor which became patently obvious when talking to the secretary of the club, is to ensure that the individual member has permission to be on the ground over which he is working.

## The Jack Russell Terrier Club of Great Britain

Just over a decade ago the Jack Russell Terrier Club was set up with the specific aim of maintaining the breed's working qualities. Because 'fun' terrier shows provide useful revenue to any organisation, whether it be a club, hunt or village society, shows soon became an important aspect to some members. This in turn led to certain disagreements between subscribers as some felt that the Jack Russell Terrier should be recognised as a true breed and be registered with the Kennel Club. Others (fortunately the majority) felt that membership of the Kennel Club could only be detrimental to the well-being of the breed.

One particular accusation often levelled at those who wish for Kennel Club recognition by those who don't is that such affiliation would result in disastrous in-breeding because this is the quickest way to establishing a certain type. Another is that, whereas it is nowadays possible to buy a Jack Russell pup for a reasonable price, once it becomes accepted as being a 'pedigree' animal, these prices will immediately double. Added to this is the fact that the actual registration of a litter of pups is bound to be more expensive. It could also be assumed that entry to shows would become more expensive.

In 1983, dissidents from the club separated and formed the minority Parson Jack Russell Club. By their own admission, they are more interested in Kennel Club recognition than they are in the terrier's working abilities and want a single showing standard of a 14 inch animal. The Jack Russell Terrier Club, however, are content to adhere to two separate heights, namely 10 inches and up to 12 inches or 12 inches and up to 15 inches (at the shoulder.)

What is particularly interesting is the fact that the man who put much of his life into founding the Jack Russell breed, namely Parson John Russell, was an initial member of the Kennel Club, which he joined in 1873. Although he remained a member until his death, he deviated when it became obvious that the club was more interested in the showing of dogs than in their working and breeding abilities. This dislike of show dogs arose from the fact that, although terriers were developed with a job of work to do, a proven show winner would be too valuable an item to risk putting down a fox or badger hole.

A point which is often forgotten by modern-day members of the Jack Russell Club no matter whether they are in favour of the breed's showing or working ability is that John Russell actually only bred a different type of fox terrier and not a separate breed. At that time, his terriers conformed to the Kennel Club specification but, as there was no breed register, his unofficial standards were open to abuse by outsiders, thereby resulting in today's separate breed. Perhaps it is worthy of mention that, until comparatively recent times, the type of terrier which the Jack Russell Terrier Club of Great Britain is keen to propagate was only seen in the areas of Devon where Jack Russell lived or in the North of England. In both places, a sturdy long-legged type was essential to cope with the difficult terrain, whereas easy digging and small holes usually found in southern areas could be managed with the short-legged, 'Queen Anne' fronted Jack Russell now only found at the end of a harness in the High Street!

Perhaps then, there is a case for the single height aimed at by the Parson Jack Russell Club – not so that they will then be eligible for membership of the Kennel Club but simply in order to arrive at a no-nonsense Jack Russell true breed. In this way much of the conflict between showing and working owners will be eliminated. It is a well-known fact amongst the working fraternity that long legs are no obstacle to a game terrier entering a hole but that crooked legs and a chest built like a barrel, are.

# Appendix 2

## THE REVEREND JOHN RUSSELL

No other individual has left as lasting an impression on the working terrier of today as the Revd John Russell. A book such as this could not, therefore, be considered complete without a very brief résumé of the man's life, environment and passion for hunting.

Born on 21 December, 1795, of a long-established Devonshire family, he was educated first at Plympton Grammar School and then at Blundells, Tiverton before becoming an undergraduate at Oxford. John's interest in hunting was fostered from early boyhood, for his father not only kept hounds but also ran a small preparatory school where the weekly reward to the pupil doing the best work was to be given the use of a small pony in order to ride to hounds.

It was whilst at Blundells, however, that his own interest in hunting became apparent and, as a result of ferreting around the local farms and thus becoming friendly with the farmers themselves, he persuaded one or two of them to allow him over their ground with his 'scratch' pack of four and a half couple of hounds which were kennelled and fed by the local blacksmith. What eventually happened to these hounds is not known but hunting them and watching the great professional huntsmen of his time whilst at Oxford, he must have picked up a great deal of knowledge which would stand him in good stead.

Stories of his days with professional packs such as the Bicester, Old Berkshire and the Duke of Beaufort's pack abound but, because of his eventual reputation, and because the stories told about him have been so often repeated, gathering embellishment with each re-telling, it is now almost impossible to verify them or trace them back to their beginnings. Undoubtedly, many of them are pure fiction while others originated in the exploits of his sporting contemporaries.

After being ordained as a priest in 1820, he took on the curacy of South Molton, just a few miles from Swimbridge where he was to spend the main part of his life. Once again he got together a small pack of hounds and 'trenchered' them amongst local inhabitants. By all accounts they were a very versatile pack and, after some initial difficulties, hunted otters in the summer, and foxes and hares in the winter. Foxes in Devonshire at that time were, however, scarce and it is recorded that in 1828 his pack found 32 foxes, killed 28 and ran 2 to ground. (With this sort of record it is perhaps not surprising that foxes were scarce!) In the same year his pack killed 73 brace of hares. By this time, mainly because of a brief amalgamation with another private pack, Russell's original scratch pack of 5 or 6 couple had grown to a pack containing 70 couple. This was, in the interests of efficiency and finance, very quickly reduced by half.

Before long the country over which he

hunted extended as far west as Cornwall and as far east as the Devon/Somerset border and every year, the Parson would take his hounds for a fortnight's hunting in Cornwall. One particular friend from this time was George Williams, who used a strain of terriers which became known as Scorrier Fox Terriers. As the development of Russell's terriers took up more and more of their originator's time, he quite frequently visited George Williams in order to pick up any draft terriers which he might have. Their friendship continued and even when Russell was 81 years of age he would still ride down to Scorrier House, a distance of 74 miles and, what is more, complete the journey in a day.

In 1833, at the age of 38, John Russell became the Vicar of Swimbridge where he remained for the next 46 years. His love of hounds, hunting and terriers continued to flourish but it must not be thought that this love made him in anyway unique as, at the same time as Russell moved to Swimbridge there were some twenty parsons in the Exeter diocese who kept their own packs of hounds, and many more who rode frequently to hounds two or three times a week.

Despite this obvious enthusiasm amongst his clergymen, the Bishop of the time, Henry Phillpots, was not at all pleased at the amount of time which his clergy spent hunting and was particularly distressed by the number who kept their own hounds. There is a story that he once tried to persuade the Reverend Russell to give up his hounds, in order to create a good example to the others. To his surprise Russell readily agreed with the words, 'Of course, if that is your wish, my Lord, I will give it up this very day,' only to follow on with, 'from tomorrow Mrs Russell will manage the pack in her name.' This reply, it might be imagined, left Bishop Phillpots sadly deflated.

From the time which he spent hunting it might be supposed that there were very few hours left in the day in which Russell could carry out his ecclesiastic duties, but nowhere can any record be found of him ever neglecting his parish or its parishioners. When he initially took on the incumbency at Swimbridge to which the neighbouring small village of Landkey was also joined, he found the parishes in a very run-down state and there was only one poorly-attended Sunday service at each church. It was not very long, however, before John Russell was himself holding four services at Swimbridge and, out of his own stipend (of £180 per annum) also managed to provide a curate by the name of Sleeman for Landkey.

The task of dealing with the inevitable hardship, poverty and sickness to be found in any rural parish in Victorian times fell largely upon the shoulders of the parson. The Reverend Russell dealt with it sympathetically, as generously as was within his means and without fuss, causing one parishioner to remark, 'He be main fond o' dogs, I allows; he likes his bottle o' port, I grants you that; but he's a proper gentleman and a Christian.'

His marriage to Penelope in 1826 proved to be a long and happy one lasting some 49 years. Her death on New Year's Day, 1875, was a bitter blow from which he never fully recovered. Their second son, Bury, (the first died whilst still in infancy) was fortunately as keen on hunting as his parents and whipped into the pack occasionally.

The Reverend John Russell followed hounds all his life and developed his own particular strain of terriers. His last resting place, in the grounds of St James's Church, Swimbridge (where he preached for 46 years), is in the heart of Devon hunting country.

The news of Russell's prowess in the hunting field eventually reached the ears of the Prince and Princess of Wales and over the ensuing years they became great friends of the Parson, inviting him to stay at Sandringham on several different occasions. In 1879, Lord Poltimore generously offered John the much more lucrative living of Black Torrington. Very reluctantly he accepted the post but wrote in a letter dated 1882:

'. . .I am getting a little more reconciled to my new home, but then it is not, and never will be Swimbridge to me.'

A year later, at the age of 88 (he was still riding to hounds until his mid-eighties) he died and, on Ascension Day, 3 May, he was brought back to Swimbridge to be buried. Such was his popularity, it was estimated that there were over a thousand people crowded into the grounds of St James's Church. His terriers provide a living memorial and the breed, unlike the words on his tombstone, is in no danger of fading away.

# Bibliography

Drabble, Phil, *Of Pedigree Unknown* (Michael Joseph, 1964)

Fell and Moorland Working Terrier Club, *The Working Terriers Handbook* (1978–1981)

Glover, Harry, *A Standard Guide to Pure-Bred Dogs* (Macmillan, 1977)

Lucas, Captain Jocelyn, *Hunt and Working Terriers* (Tide-line, 1979)

Parkes, Charlie and Thornley, John, *Fair Game* (Pelham, 1987)

Porter, Val, *Faithful Companions* (Pelham, 1987)

Russell, Dan, *Jack Russell and his Terriers* (J.A. Allen, 1979)

Smith, Guy N., *Sporting and Working Dogs* (Saiga, 1979)

Sparrow, Geoffrey, *The Terrier's Vocation* (J.A. Allen, 1961)

Spottiswoode, J., *The Moorland Gamekeeper* (David and Charles, 1977)

Willoughby, The Hon. Charles, *Come and Hunt* (Museum Press, 1952)

# Index